```
DT
107.828    Narayan, Brij Kumar, 1922-
S23            Anwar el Sadat
N37
```

WITHDRAWN

980 Fremont Blvd.
Monterey, California 93940

ANWAR EL SADAT

ANWAR EL SADAT
Man with a Mission

COL. B.K. NARAYAN

VIKAS PUBLISHING HOUSE PVT LTD
New Delhi Bombay Bangalore Calcutta Kanpur

VIKAS PUBLISHING HOUSE PVT LTD
5 Ansari Road, New Delhi 110002
Savoy Chambers, 5 Wallace Street, Bombay 400001
10 First Main Road, Gandhi Nagar, Bangalore 560009
8/1-B Chowringhee Lane, Calcutta 700016
80 Canning Road, Kanpur 208004

Copyright © Col. B.K. NARAYAN, 1977

ISBN 0 7069 0490 7

1V02N2001

Rs 35

Printed at Delhi Press, Jhandewalan, New Delhi

Foreword

I welcome the opportunity to pen a few introductory lines about this brief biography of President Anwar el Sadat. The book seeks to present to the interested students of modern Egyptian history a few facets of the personality of the Egyptian President in the context of the various historical forces operating in the sensitive theatre of West Asia and the way he faced the various challenges, more particularly since he assumed presidency after the death of Gamal Abdel Nasser.

I recall the early days at the Military Academy in Cairo which produced such outstanding officers as Nasser and Sadat who were to make an imprint on the national and international scene in subsequent years. One would normally consider as rather premature, a biography of a political leader who is still very much active on the domestic and international stage, but in this case such an effort needs no apology since what President Sadat has achieved in the short span of nearly six years of presidency already assures him a place in history. These years have been action-packed years, full of travail, suffering, hard work, tough decisions, faith, and dedication. Seldom is it given to a leader to achieve so much in so little time. Sadat rescued the nation from the quagmire of despondency and demoralisation and restored it to its dignity and role of destiny.

Those early contacts and my subsequent relationship with

President Sadat in my various official capacities created certain indelible impressions in my mind about his personal characteristics, style, and approach to life. The dominant impression one gathers on meeting Sadat is that he is simple, unostentatious, friendly, loyal and calm. His friendliness and goodwill are palpable. Similarly, he displays an unruffled calm in the face of crises and exudes confidence. He does not jump to conclusions but is deliberate and reflects deeply on issues before according decisions. While arriving at a decision he listens to all aspects of the case and all points of view bearing on the problem. He is a patient listener and listens more than he speaks. This does not, however, mean that he cannot give quick decisions when the situation demands it. Far from it. He is unambiguous and forthright in giving his decisions. Sadat, even while at the Military College, stood out from among the common run of students. His mode of speech had its own stamp, clear and distinct and shorn of all ambiguity.

Sadat has a distinct rural background and has deep roots in the soil. He understands the mass of his people like the palm of his hand. His high office has not changed his innate simplicity. When he visits his village he merges into its environ naturally, displaying respect for elders and their cherished values. He is humble and shuns pomp and pride. Like an Egyptian farmer he is simple, strong, hardworking, respectful, and deliberate in his actions. He has no complexes. Sadat has a democratic approach and prefers a thorough discussion and a collective assessment of the situation. He gives weight to every viewpoint so that the decision arrived at is based on a consensus.

When I was Ambassador in Peking, Sadat led a delegation to China. At that time he was the Speaker of the National Assembly. When I went to visit him, he was dressed in his flowing Egyptian rural robe and was reading a book. On seeing me he asked me to sit by him on his couch very informally. His simple dress and informality attracted notice. Later when he visited Mongolia he was presented with a robe at a public function. He was very happy with the gift and donned it on the spot. The audience was thrilled. Sadat was in his elements. His informality had established a rapport between him and his audience at once.

When Nasser died suddenly on 28 September 1970, an indescribable gloom descended on the Arab horizon in general and the

Egyptian scene in particular. The future was a big question mark. The prophets of doom were full of forebodings. The ship of state was seemingly rudderless. The Arabs were in a state of disarray. Egypt was still reeling under the blows received in June 1967. The economy was on the verge of collapse. The nation had lost its confidence. There were problems galore but no solutions.

Sadat faced some very difficult days before the Ramadan War of October 1973. There were student demonstrations, manoeuvres, and plots against him but he was not easily ruffled and endured everything with patience until his mind was made up. Once clear about how to tackle the situation, he took decisive action and nipped all anti-national conspiracies in the bud. He took the unpalatable but necessary legal action against conspirators such as Ali Sabri and others, and ordered their trial in a court of law so that every one had a fair chance of defending himself. Sadat, however, showed his attachment to humanitarian principles and his deep faith in justice and fairplay. He ensured that the families and the dependants of the arrested persons did not suffer in any manner, financially and otherwise. They continued to receive their shares as of old. Sadat's solicitude in this respect is due to the fact that he himself had gone through periods of severe trials and tribulations in his political career when he was being hounded from pillar to post by the British security authorities, and for some time he even worked as a driver incognito. This explains his extreme concern for and anxiety to provide social security to the Egyptian masses to cover loss of employment, old age, and disease.

Impartial observers have already conceded that Sadat was the prime force behind forging Arab unity prior to the Ramadan War. His decision to cross the Canal and challenge the lion in his own den was fraught with danger and the consequences could have been disastrous had there been the slightest leakage in intelligence or any lapse in planning. It certainly ranks as a great decision in history. The elaborate preparations which he undertook before executing his plan went to show his extreme concern for the lives of the brave sons of Egypt who were being called upon to make the supreme sacrifice.

On 16 October 1973, Sadat delivered an important speech in which he stated that the Arabs had fought for the sake of peace, a peace which was based on justice, because peace which was imposed and which was not based on justice had no permanence.

It was only peace with justice which could change the course of history, put an end to centuries of backwardness and defeat, and open the Arab horizons to a new morrow, shedding its lustre over all Arab lands. The battles for peace were more exacting and more demanding than the battles with weapons and equipment.

Sadat's view of life is a comprehensive one. Life according to him is not to be divided into water-tight compartments. In his view the development of the individual as a whole was involved where there was a perfect balance between body and mind on the one hand and the mind and the soul on the other. No aspect of life, whether politics or any other, could be excluded from the total aspect of a balanced human personality and it was only such sure foundations which could inspire a whole generation to make correct decisions and react to events on the national and international scene with courage, competence, and balance.

An outstanding trait of Sadat is his imperturbability and calm in the face of difficulties, hostilities and challenges. He is not easily shaken, nor can he be bamboozled into hasty or panicky action. His decisions are arrived at after mature thought. Once made, they are his own firm decisions. They have paid rich dividends in the past. The book seeks to provide background information on Sadat the man, his ideas, and his methods. I have pleasure in commending the book.

ZAKARIA ADLY IMAM
Ambassador Extraordinary and Plenipotentiary of the Arab Republic of Egypt in India

Preface

Sadat has emerged on the political horizon of West Asia as the foremost Arab leader, whose actions and decisions have triggered a whole series of political, military and economic consequences affecting West Asia in particular and the world in general. He has forced the super powers to modify the framework of detente to take into account the West Asian crisis. He has forced a reappraisal of U.S. policy vis-a-vis West Asia. It was his initiative which made the Arabs conscious of their oil power and reap economic benefits in astronomical figures. He gave a new perspective to third world politics. Many facts still shrouded in the folds of secrecy when brought to surface in due course will perhaps prove that President Sadat has never compromised with basic Arab demands nor has he abdicated his freedom of action vis-a-vis the super powers.

The referendum held in 1970 gave Sadat a massive mandate of six million votes as against seven hundred thousand. Today he would sweep the polls with near unanimity. Those who witnessed the spontaneous and tumultuous welcome accorded to him in November 1975 on his return from the USA will cherish it as a memorable experience. Sadat's stature has steadily grown with time and it will continue to grow if the present is any indication.

Sadat is every inch an Egyptian—simple, friendly and hospitable. He has achieved immense popularity among his people, and is never too busy to spend an afternoon with the family of a soldier killed in the Ramadan War, or to attend the funeral of his old teacher of his childhood days back in his village. These are not contrived gestures but spontaneous expressions of a basically simple and honest person whose loyalties are genuine and deep. Gratitude and loyalty are inherent in his make-up.

I am grateful of H.E. Zakaria Adly Imam, the Ambassador of the Arab Republic of Egypt in India, who has been a close colleague and comrade of the Egyptian President, for his valuable foreword, and I was able to gather useful information from my conversations with him. I hope this book will not only help in understanding one of the leading statesmen of our time but will also build bridges of understanding between Egypt and the rest of the world.

B. K. NARAYAN

Contents

1. Introduction 1
2. The Years of Agony 13
3. The Early Years and the War College 23
4. The Free Officers Take the Plunge 32
5. Dawn of Revolution 44
6. In Defence of the Revolution 52
7. Sadat Blazes a New Trail 59
8. Vital Decisions 77
9. War and its Aftermath 91
10. The Path of the Golden Mean 104
11. Egypt's First Lady 121
12. In Sadat's Words 126
13. Some Objections Reviewed 137
14. The Future 143
    Appendices 151
    Select Bibliography 155
    Index 157

"History is nothing but a constant humbling of arrogance."

Anwar el Sadat in
REVOLT ON THE NILE

1

Introduction

"He lay lifeless on his bed, moving only when the electric shock machinery sent three charges quivering through his body. It was hoped that the shocks would start his heart beating again. But nothing would restart Gamal Abdel Nasser's heart. It was broken."

"As the hopelessness of the doctors communicated itself to the men standing round the room they began to display the first signs of that great wave of grief that roared through the Arab world."

"Anwar el Sadat who was to succeed Nasser, stood by the bed, turned his face to heaven and recited verses from the Qoran." This is how Mohammed Heikal described the passing of Nasser and the traumatic events of 28 September 1970 in his book *Nasser—The Cairo Documents*. The verses recited by Sadat were inscribed on Nasser's tomb:

> "*O ye tranquil soul*
> *Return back to your God willingly and you are accepted,*
> *Return back to my house among the faithful.*"

"Then Vice-President Sadat told the world the news in a short broadcast. The effect was both instantaneous and fantastic. People poured out of their houses into the night and made their way to the broadcasting station on the banks of the Nile to find out if what they had heard was true. It is strange that since time immemorial the Egyptian people are always drawn to the Nile at moments of extreme emotion and that night the methods of modern communication coincided with their age-old feelings."

"First there were little groups to be seen in the streets, then hundreds, then thousands, then tens of thousands and then the streets were black with people and it was impossible for anybody to move. A group of women outside the broadcasting station were screaming. 'The Lion is dead,' they cried, 'the Lion is dead.' It was a cry that came to echo round Cairo and it spread through the villages until it filled Egypt. That night and in the days to come he was mourned with a wild and passionate grief. Soon people began to move into Cairo from all parts of Egypt until there were ten million in the city. The authorities stopped the trains running for there was nowhere for the people to stay and food supplies were running short. But still they came, by car, by donkey, and on foot."

As fate would have it, it was the voice of Sadat which announced the Egyptian revolution of 23 July 1952 to the world over the Cairo radio. Sadat had now assumed control of the Republic according to the provisions of the constitution. He did so without fuss or ceremony. He seemed to naturally assume the mantle cast on his shoulders by history. He has not looked back since and his decisions have had a profound effect on the course of events in West Asia and the world at large.

Three years had passed since the death of Nasser. It was now 6 October 1973. It was Sadat who launched the Egyptian armed forces across the Suez Canal on that historic day. He described the day as follows in his *Memoirs*:

> On 6 October (10 Ramadan) I woke up after a calm night during which I had a deep sleep and in the morning I followed the usual programme. I started with physical exercises I was accustomed to since I was in prison. I believe that there should be a balance between mind, body and soul so that a man may lead a sound life and adopt a balanced behaviour which affects all decisions which one takes.
>
> My mind was very active and was ready to shoulder the responsibilities of the new day. My soul was praying in silence for the day on which Egypt would cross the barrier of silence, fear,

terror and defeatism. We were determined to overcome all obstacles in the way of our march and all my calculations indicated that we would win whatever the consequences.

At 1.20 p.m. General Ahmed Ismail called on me as agreed upon and we both drove in an army jeep to the operations room or 'Centre No. 10' which was well equipped with the latest gadgets to establish contact with any part of Egypt even if the telephone or wireless contact was cut off. I arrived at the operations room at 1.30 p.m. and greeted the commanders who were standing before their maps. As it was Ramadan I was fasting as usual because I was accustomed to fasting since my childhood. The people of the village considered fasting a sign of manhood and ever since my childhood I did not break the fast under any pretext. Fasting, faith, religion, praying and belief have become one indivisible entity and I feel that if the balance between them is upset one would surrender a part of himself and his balance. I gave instructions that all should break the fast so that there might not be any chance whatsoever of committing an error or forgetting any detail as a result of fasting. This was necessary in the case of particularly those who were used to smoking or drinking tea. I therefore ordered a cup of tea, and my pipe to be brought from the car. This relieved the commanders of any embarrassment and they followed suit.

Sadat has made his mark on the international stage as the standard-bearer of Arab action. It is, therefore, necessary to put the personality of Sadat in a proper historical perspective for a better understanding of contemporary Egypt and the Arab world. The historical background of Egypt and the personality of Sadat are interrelated as they represent two sides of the same coin. Egypt represents a very ancient and a very rich civilization. It has fought countless wars and has absorbed and imbibed many strains of culture. It is not only the most modern and the most politically conscious Arab country but also bears on its shoulders the responsibility for setting the pace for pan-Arab action. Egypt can neither opt out of Arab leadership nor can the Arabs in general do without Egypt. The importance of Egypt's strategic location is out of all proportion to its size or population. Destiny seems to have chosen Egypt for a very special role for which she pays a heavy price.

In the aftermath of the First World War there was consolidation by British imperialism of its hold over Egypt. This phase was the harbinger of an emergent nationalism which was soon to grip the entire country. The Second World War brought about the Egyptian freedom movement to its final stage of consummation. The decadent imperialist power exhausted by the protracted war and a shattered economy was no longer in a position to stem the rising tide of nationalism in Egypt. The Egyptian army officers fired with the zeal of liberating their land from the yoke of British imperialism tried to establish contact with the Germans. The Axis success in the northern desert and the Allied setbacks encouraged this where the Italian and German forces were knocking at the gates of Mersa Matruh.

Shortly after the end of the Second World War the glorious revolution of 23 July 1952 was staged in Egypt. The British reacted to it like a drowning man clutching at a straw. While on the one hand it encouraged fissiparous tendencies within the national body politic of Egypt, on the other it tried to foment trouble by sponsoring military pacts such as the Baghdad Pact to divide the Arab world. Alarmed by the Egyptian revolution the imperialists engineered the tripartite Anglo-French-Israeli aggression on Egypt hoping that the Egyptian leadership would collapse by its weight. What happened was quite the reverse. The entire Egyptian nation stood like one man and it was the tripartite conspiracy that collapsed. The imperialists waited for another eleven years before they dealt a deadly blow to Egypt in 1967. Sadat had thus inherited the legacy of a defeated army and a demoralised people unsure of themselves.

The super powers were committed to the territorial integrity and national survival of Israel and no major war could erupt or continue for long except within a limited framework. Sadat's effort was to precisely assess the limits to which the super powers would go in supporting the respective sides in defence of their global interests. He embarked on the decision to go to war in October 1973 much against the overt and covert wishes of the Soviet Union and the USA. It was thus a positive and independent strategy that Sadat pursued which was not only militarily successful, but also forced the super powers to disclose their cards.

He realised more than anyone else how countries which were dependent on the super powers for their weapons were at the mercy of these powers when the hostilities ensued. The detente between the two super powers had not filtered down to cover the other areas of the world, many of which were seething with unrest and an explosive discontent. The detente could not rule out zonal and regional confrontations. It was this which forced Sadat to call a halt to hostilities when the political purpose of launching the war had been achieved, i.e. defreezing the Middle Eastern situation and providing a spark to usher in a new era of political, military, economic and social relationships in the world by giving a new turn to history through the uniquely bold decision to cross the Suez Canal.

If the State of Israel was to be guaranteed within the pre-1967 borders by the super powers, then the Arab-Israeli confrontation should be well-tailored to yield political results. Sadat, therefore, declared that he was not going to fight the USA by proxy. If the dissolution of the state of Israel was to be ruled out, it was necessary to bring about a basic change in the political and economic environment to force a reappraisal on the part of the super powers about the scope and extent of their support to it. The Ramadan War made the super powers realise the need for a fresh appreciation of their national interest by recognising the need for establishing a new relationship with the Arab world and recast the role of Israel in protecting their interests and determining the degree of their support to her in the light of new realities.

It was no mere accident that Sadat was chosen as the man of the year in 1975 by *Time* magazine whereas Sadat himself called 1975 the year of Palestine. In its issue of 5 January 1976 *Time* magazine stated in its European edition that Sadat had distinguished himself not only by his realism and moderation but also by displaying an abundant confidence in his own power. When the voice of Sadat announced the advent of the 23 July 1952 revolution over the Cairo radio, his voice was clear, confident, remarkably unruffled and calm. Immediately after the announcement he returned to the Revolutionary Command Council which was waiting for him. They were waiting so that they could take appropriate action in case anything went wrong. Those who lived those glorious moments remember with pride and nostalgia the turning point in the history of Egypt. It was the same Sadat who was sent for by Nasser in December 1969 before the latter was leaving for Morocco to attend the Arab summit and asked to take the oath of office as Vice-President. Again it was Sadat who alone was asked to be present along with other military leaders when the Egyptian Defence Plan 200 was being discussed by a very select group of officers.

Sadat is not known for swimming with the current. Indeed he has shown his penchant for taking unpalatable decisions. One may argue with him but none may question his patriotism, his dedication to the Arab cause, or his statesmanship. One may question his methods but never his ends. His worst enemies will not deny him the credit for bringing about far-reaching changes on the Arab and the international scene by his momentous decision to go to war. He was equally firm later in following the path of moderation and seeking a political settlement. For the first time in history, before the Ramadan War so many divergent views in the Arab world were brought together on one platform. He continues to play a unifying role wherever and whenever the Arab ranks show signs of internal discord and friction whether it be Lebanon, the Sahara, or the Gulf. His heart bleeds for the Arabs when they show an inadequate realisation of their own tremendous potentials—unlimited wealth, enormous oil resources, control over the vital routes of communication, one language, and a homogeneous culture.

A few critics even within the Arab world have rushed to label Sadat either pro-West or anti-Soviet whereas Sadat has himself never functioned in a stereotyped fashion accepting these epithets. In the pursuit of his ideals he adopts the methods and means best suited to yield the desired results. To the people of the Indian sub-continent Sadat is not a stranger. It is not perhaps widely known that Sadat interceded with Bhutto on behalf of Sheikh Mujib ur Rehman and saved him from the gallows. During his whirlwind tour of India, Pakistan, and Bangla Desh in February 1974, he did what he could to bring about a climate of understanding and conciliation in the sub-continent. His moderation and sense of balance have acted as a healing balm at Islamic summit conferences. Much of his valuable contribution to the non-aligned countries has been made through work behind the scenes.

Introduction

It would be natural in the current-day world to assess a politician in terms of gains and losses vis-a-vis his policies and actions. It would not be out of place to list a few of Sadat's achievements. He restored to the Arabs their dignity on the sands of Sinai. He stormed the Israelis over the East Bank defences on the Canal and ultimately secured the vital Gidi and Mitla passes. He deprived the Israeli war machine of the oil supplies from Abu Rudeis. He made the Arabs conscious of their oil power through their joint exercise of this power as a weapon. He opened the international waterway of the Suez Canal to give an impetus to East-West trade and a new economic world over. He compelled the West to accord formal recognition to the Palestinian national rights by urging them to invite the Palestinian representatives to participate in the various UN meetings and specialised agencies. He also gave the producers of raw materials an opportunity to realise their strength and galvanise themselves into action to demand a more equitable treatment at the hands of the advanced industrial nations. He re-established man's faith in the fundamental values of true religion and morality in the domain of social action. This is but a brief catalogue of the harvest which Sadat's policies have already yielded.

If there was no progress towards the consummation of the political goal of the Arabs, Sadat reckoned that militarily he would be in a better position with the vital Gidi and Mitla passes in Arab rather than Israeli hands. Sadat realised only too well that it was not only Egypt which had a stake in the continued functioning of the Canal but also Europe, Asia, and Africa, whose trade and economy were largely dependent on the continued operation of the Canal. Sadat thus enlisted the support of the international community against exposing the waterway to the caprices of a recalcitrant enemy. The Egyptian control of the passes no doubt ensures the physical security of the Canal. Sadat is judiciously using the current phase for initiating both short-term and long-term plans for the rearmament of Egypt. Incomplete preparation and inadequate execution of half-baked plans can only damage the Arab cause and result in the demoralisation of the Arab troops. Sadat would not hurl the Arab forces with indifferent equipment and inadequate preparation into another trial of strength in an irresponsible manner, and risk his men and material against the re-armed, refitted and re-equipped Israeli forces.

Preparation for war did not mean mere acquisition of a number of weapons and equipment, however advanced. This had to take place against the background of internal and external unity and a sound economic base which could sustain the stresses and strains of war. It was in pursuance of this that Sadat took the unpleasant step of liquidating various power centres which sapped national energy and weakened the collective will of the nation. It was again for this purpose that he undertook repeated travels to the various Arab countries rich and poor, to build a solid economic and political base for Arab action. He undertook to implement certain long-term measures to improve the capacity of the country to produce modern weapons and equipment with foreign collaboration, in the knowledge and belief that the coming generations would have a solid foundation to build on. He did not leave scope for people to say that long-term Arab interests were sacrificed for temporary gains.

When Sadat took over as the President six years ago, those occupying the seats of power and authority in Cairo were unaware of his hidden potential. However, it did not take long for these persons to realise that he was a man of steel and not a pliable and soft person they could utilise for their own ends. They also wanted to make Sadat the scapegoat for policy legacies the country had inherited from the past. On 13 May 1971, when the members of the group (or the centres of power as they were referred to) tendered their collective resignation, Sadat did not find it difficult to deal with the situation. The members were promptly arrested and brought to trial and a new government was formed under Aziz Sidki. This was the first bold decision Sadat took on the assumption of office. Though he effectively dealt with this group of entrenched politicians he still had to build his power base. He had to utilise the existing machinery for this purpose, viz. the Arab Socialist Union. He started by reorganising this union. It was inevitable that the union was purged of entrenched elements who were connected with or committed to not policies but discredited personalities involved in the mass resignation.

Curiously, events were happening in the Sudan at this very time where coup-makers were challenging Jaffar Numeiri's rule. Sadat rushed to the support of Jaffar Numeiri in ensuring that no externally-inspired elements were allowed to topple his regime. In order to strengthen Numeiri's hands, Sadat even relieved the

Sudanese army contingent from the Canal zone to return home. The failure of the coup against Numeiri in the Sudan and the liquidation of the power centres in Egypt created a new situation which indicated for the first time that Sadat had a mind of his own and could effectively intercede or intervene in pursuance of his independent policies. This turn of events could not have pleased the Soviets, but during the latter half of 1971 despite many mutual visits between Soviet and Egyptian leaders, the interests of the two sides had begun to diverge. The Soviet presence in Egypt at that time was considerable, though not quite popular with the Egyptian army ranks.

1972 witnessed a progress of detente between the Soviet Union and the USA and this could not be called exactly helpful to a solution of the West Asian crisis. Neither the USA nor the Soviet Union could afford to jeopardise detente by promoting a conflagration in West Asia. A status quo suited them, but not Sadat. Hitherto Egypt had been reacting to situations forced on her but now Sadat wanted to wrest the initiative and force the super powers to react to his moves instead. Nevertheless, he had to postpone the year of decision in 1971 and 1972. Looking back through the other end of the telescope it is easier now to appreciate the dilemmas which Sadat faced then. Sadat's repeated attempts to obtain ground-to-ground missiles and the advanced Migs 23 did not meet with a favourable response from the Soviet Union. Perhaps the combat readiness of the Egyptian army and its technical competence was doubted by the Soviet Union. They were chary of committing their advanced offensive weapons. Despite these setbacks Sadat had made up his mind and was biding time to execute his plans at an opportune moment. He visited Moscow in April 1972. This visit was interpreted by the Soviet Union to obtain leverage in their talks with the US leaders by pretending that the Arabs laid great store by Soviet support.

President Assad of Syria visited Cairo on 9 July 1972 to convey to Sadat that in the Soviet view the Arabs should think twice before starting a war. It was clear that 1972 could not be a year of decision. Indeed it was widely believed in both eastern and western circles that Sadat would not continue in office for long. The situation in the Arab world generally was unsatisfactory. The war in Jordan, in which Jordanian forces were involved with the Palestinians, had brought about a further disarray in the Arab ranks.

Against this background, and the passing of Nasser, Israel was in no mood to give serious consideration to Jarrings' proposals or to any other serious peace proposals at all. She had turned arrogant.

Thinking the Egyptian position to be militarily and politically weak, Moshe Dayan made a suggestion that the Israeli forces move 20 miles east of the Suez Canal to enable the Egyptian authorities to open it for international traffic. Dayan's calculation was that once the Canal was opened, both the Russians as well as the Egyptians would develop a vested interest in keeping it open and keep the zone free of conflict. Whereas the proposal was rejected by Sadat outright, it did not receive any encouragement from the USA either. Sadat realised that such an interim measure would freeze the situation once again and rob the problem of its urgency. The U.S. interests were not served by the opening of the Suez Canal. Only the Soviet Union would gain an easier access to the Gulf and the Indian Ocean. Sadat, however, let it be known that he was neither against detente nor was he interested in sabotaging U.S.-Soviet rapprochement but that the West Asian crisis was being put into cold storage, a development which he could not countenance.

Sadat informed the National Assembly in early 1973 that he had become the Chief Executive only to prepare the country for war against Israel. He reckoned that the Israelis still enjoyed a two-to-one superiority and within the Arab fold no unified Arab plans could be hatched except with Syria, for security reasons. Against this background, Sadat's decision to go to war in October 1973 was a surprise move by any standards.

A remarkable rapport was established by Sadat with the late King Feisal, a relationship which survives in the friendship of Sadat and King Khalid. The shrewd King Feisal had lately witnessed many unwelcome developments all round Saudi Arabia. The developments in South Yemen, the Iraqi-Soviet friendship pact, and the revolt in the Dhofar province of Oman were events which could not have been to the liking of the late Saudi monarch. Sadat's carefully calculated move found a ready echo in King Feisal's whole-hearted endorsement. The enormous funds and the money power at his disposal was a very strong pivot on which Egyptian-Saudi collaboration could achieve almost miraculous results, signifying a break from the past and projecting a new

Introduction

outlook for the future.

Sitting on the crossroads of the world, Sadat was in a unique position to influence the course of events affecting the East, the West, the non-aligned, the Afro-Asian, the Arab, the non-Arab, and the Third World in an intimate manner. It was not possible to ignore what he said or did. The personality of Sadat commanded compelling attention because of his sincerity and strength of purpose. He had taken unpalatable decisions which only the future could judge. Sadat had made it abundantly clear that whatever the compulsions and limitations, he would never forsake or abandon the basic Arab causes. There could be no compromise on the Israeli withdrawal from occupied Arab territories. Any Israeli attack on Syria would invite Egyptian reprisals and a renewed struggle for Palestinian national rights to be recognised. On these basic attitudes there was to be no going back or retraction. All that he has insisted on is that a political and peaceful solution should be given a fair chance to succeed. The fact that some very venomous attacks have been levelled against him by fellow-Arabs has neither affected his judgement nor left any trace of bitterness in him on this account. No Arab leader, let alone Sadat, is in a position today to opt out of war as long as the basic Arab goals are not achieved. Arab force acting as a deterrent can alone control Israeli misadventures, and this deterrent has to be carefully built and guarded. It is therefore vital that there be amity between fellow Arabs.

On the war front, the destruction of the Barlev Line leaves Israel with no other defensible feature unless she thinks of establishing another defensive line practically three times the size and length of the Barlev Line. The Canal traffic is no longer under the nose of the Israelis. Sadat has eliminated Egyptian dependence on a single source for weapons and equipment, thus eliminating the political debt which such dependence silently creates. According to Kissinger "the limited agreement between Egypt and Israel has 'contributed' to the general improvement of relations between the two nuclear super powers because neither of them wanted the area to trigger a global war. . . ."

There really is no cause for feeling alarmed over the Sinai disengagement agreement. The disengagement agreement did not terminate the state of war. The termination of the state of war depends on a rapid political progress which alone can lead to a peace treaty. Sadat did not agree to the passage of any military commodities for Israel through the Suez Canal but permitted only the carriage of non-military commodities in non-Israeli ships in accordance with the 1882 Constantinople Convention. Even this was conditional upon peace prevailing in the area because the Constantinople Convention itself would be null and void in case of an outbreak of war.

2

The Years of Agony

As one thinks of Egypt, one's mind is instantly transported to the vision of the timeless pyramids which stand as eternal signposts on the cross-roads of the world. Over five thousand years ago the Egyptian civilisation had reached heights the comprehension of which defies the intelligence of twentieth century men. To visit Egypt is to take a peep into the eternity of space and time. The modern Egyptian has a rich legacy of the Pharaohnic history which lasted for 3,500 years. This was followed by an invasion by Alexander in the 4th century B.C. introducing the Greek civilization into Egypt. The Greco-Roman period lasted a 1000 years when Christianity generally prevailed in Egypt, particularly during the latter part of the period. It was in the seventh century that the Arab-Islamic civilization made its enduring appearance and has flourished ever since. Egypt has great monuments pertaining to each phase of her chequered history which hold one spell-bound.[1]

In the west of the city of Cairo stand the magnificent pyramids, in the south some of the oldest churches of Christendom, and in the north and in the city numerous mosques with the pride of place going to the mosques of Amr and Ibn Tulun which are of great architectural elegance. The Arab Islamic character of Egypt was established unmistakably with the coming of the Fatimids

---

[1]For further details see *Encyclopaedia Britannica*, Vol. 8, 1957, pp 56-73.

and with the laying of the foundation of the city of Cairo on 5 August 969.

Though the Muslim Arabs conquered Egypt in the year 640 it was governed by different ruling houses at different periods, some independently and some under the authority of the Caliph of Baghdad. Among the independent ruling families were the Fatimids who held power from 969 to 1171. After the Fatimids the Ayyubis were the rulers whose dynasty was founded by Saladin al Ayyubi. Saladin achieved great fame in the Crusades which was not merely a clash between two religious but basically a conflict between two patterns of culture. Saladin's citadel is one of the distinguished landmarks of Cairo. The Ayoubid dynasty whose foundation was laid by Saladin held power from 1171 to 1250. A slave dynasty which originally owed allegiance to the Ayyubid dynasty later captured power independently and was known as the Mameluk. The Mameluk rule lasted until 1517 when the Ottoman conquest took place.

Throughout the centuries Egypt has faced the challenges of history and geography with courage and continued in a state of perpetual struggle with a glorious record of sacrifices in blood and Herculean effort. Her thirsty sands have, nevertheless, proved to be the graveyard of invaders whatever their momentary swings of fortune. The people of Egypt have stood like a rock while the caravan of history has marched onwards with a relentless force. She has always remained conscious of her greatness, the greatness of her ancient traditions, her spirit of indomitable resistance and her love of independence.

The Ottoman conquest of Egypt in 1517 resulted in a complete devastation of her national resources in manpower and skilled artisans who were mercilessly whisked away to Turkey. This period saw a rapid depletion of Egyptian resources and five centuries of harsh and cruel rule by the Mameluks left Egypt impoverished. The Mameluks were a slave dynasty who wielded power though outwardly they recognised Turkish authority. Chronologically, they followed the empires of Saladin and the Fatimids whose glorious relics adorn the Egypt of today.

In 1798, when Napoleon entered Egypt, he was shocked to find that she was depleted of her wealth beyond description. Napoleon's entry into Egypt exposed her to the European civilisation. That was also the time when the sea route to India via the Cape was discovered, which resulted in a further weakening of the Egyptian economy. Until then the commercial route linking the far east with Europe passed through the Red Sea, then overland between Suez and Alexandria and to Europe by sea. Egypt thus lost heavily in transit charges accruing to her at the time of entrance, during transit, and at the time of exit of goods across her soil.*

When Napoleon ended the Ottoman rule over Egypt, he really aimed a dagger (great strategist that he was) at the British hold on their eastern empire. The British, the dominant sea power, were sensitive to the French move and lost no time in sending their fleet under Nelson who destroyed the French ships at Alexandria while Napoleon's forces were busy fighting inside Cairo on the outskirts of the Pyramids and the Sphinx. The French were thus blockaded and forced to retire from Egypt in the year 1801. The French had also brought along with them a number of scholars, engineers, architects and craftsmen. It is a tribute to Napoleon's genius that when he looked at the deserts of Egypt on the one hand and at the Nile on the other, he felt that not a single drop of the Nile should lose itself in the Mediterranean. Once again it was the expert team which Napoleon was carrying with him in this expedition which thought of an initial plan for joining the Red Sea with the Mediterranean through the Suez Canal.

It was again the French who introduced the Arabic printing press for the first time in Egypt. The French withdrawal from Egypt gave a chance to the British to bring Egypt back under Turkish rule under Mohammed Ali, an Albanian soldier who was put in the lead. The Mameluks were, at that time, a force within Egypt and Mohammed Ali was fearful of their power. He, however, engineered a clever plot by which he got the entire group of Mameluks massacred inside the citadel and thus consolidated his regime.

---

*History repeated itself in 1967 when the Suez Canal was closed and the Cape route was restored to its ancient importance and prosperity at the expense of Egypt. Sadat reversed this retrograde development by opening the Suez Canal both to rehabilitate world trade as well as to usher in prosperity for Egypt. He took the bold and necessary steps to ensure the security of the Suez Canal by occupying the Gidi and Mitla passes east of the Canal through a combination of military and diplomatic means, and secured the western parts of the Sinai to ensure the safety and security of the Canal traffic against the vagaries of political and military fortunes in this sensitive area of the world.

Mohammed Ali realised that he had to depend on the Egyptian soldiery to organise his army and not on the Turkish elements on whose behalf he had been appointed a Viceroy. Hitherto under Turkish rule the Egyptians had been deprived of the opportunity of enlisting in the army and training as soldiers. The Egyptian farmers were in most cases forcibly recruited as labourers. The Army was taboo for them. Mohammed Ali had to make a departure from this tradition and introduce mass education to enable Egyptian farmers to have a smattering of literacy before they entered the army. With the army thus reconstituted he fought the Wahabis and extended his domain as far as Mecca and Medina. Sudan was also conquered by him in 1823. This phase of conquest continued until 1832 when his ambition took him to Constantinople. It was here that he met his Waterloo at the hands of the British who forced him to quit Syria and Arabia. He became the viceroy of Egypt in 1841 and died in 1849.

Mohammed Ali's contribution was notable in Egyptian history because the army which he led was composed of Egyptians and it only proved that the Egyptian soldier was good fighting material provided that manoeuvers were planned and ably led, a fact which was proved in October 1973 when Sadat took the historic decision of crossing the Suez Canal and challenging the Israeli forces in their den. Mohammed Ali laid the foundation of an Egyptianised army, a tradition which has continued to flourish since and on whose shoulders has fallen the mantle of providing leadership to the Arab world as a whole. Both strategically, equipment-wise and training-wise, the reorganised Egyptian army of post-1967 vintage is by far the most competent and important fighting force in the Arab world and West Asia today.

Mohammed Ali also introduced cotton into Egypt for the first time. In order to provide water for this crop during summer, a dam was planned in the area of the delta so that the level of the Nile could be brought up. The dam was commissioned only in 1883.

In 1854 another event of great consequence occurred. Khedive Said of Egypt, the grandson of Mohammed Ali, granted a license to Ferdinand de Lesseps, a Frenchman, to dig a canal to link the Red Sea with the Mediterranean. Ironically the people who opposed the digging of a canal at that stage were none other than the British who felt that the French might establish an empire in

Egypt thus threatening the British sea route to the east. Historically it would be interesting to know that in the year 640 Amr Ibn al Aas had constructed a canal joining the Red Sea to the Nile but its main purpose was to send wheat to drought-stricken Arabia. Nevertheless, the approval was given, the initial hurdles were overcome, and work on the canal began in 1859.

Unfortunately, the signed contract was so cleverly worded that the digging of the canal became a colossal liability for Egypt in terms of manpower resources and expenses. 25,000 workers were provided by Egypt and they were subjected to inhuman conditions of work, so harsh that every three months thousands died and the force had to be renewed. It is estimated that nearly 120,000 workers died in digging the canal, a terrible price which Egypt was made to pay by virtue of her geographical and strategic position. 75 per cent of the Suez Canal Company shares belonged to the management, and the contract which was signed with the Egyptian government was to last ninety-nine years. In 1869 the Suez Canal was formally opened to the accompaniment of merrymaking which cost the Egyptian coffers $12 million. Not only had Egypt lost thousands of her workers, but the terms of contract had practically rendered her bankrupt. Ismail, the monarch of Egypt between 1863 and 1879, became the bankrupt. Khedive who was forced to apply for foreign loans to meet treaty obligations, an event which opened the floodgates of intrigue and interference of outsiders in Egyptian affairs. The conditions attached to these loans were such that Ismail had to sell the Egyptian shares of the Suez Canal Company which were only 15 per cent. These shares were sold to Britain for £4 million. Within three years of this transaction Egypt's debts increased to £68 million through manipulation. Having lost even the shares of the Company, Ismail was left bankrupt with a huge debt hanging over his head and the gates of Egypt were thrown wide open for Anglo-French intervention in Egyptian governmental affairs. Ismail abdicated in favour of his son Tewfik, a stooge in the hands of his Anglo-French masters. This state of affairs led to extreme dissatisfaction in the ranks of the Egyptian army, a development which was to bear fruit in 1952 with far-reaching consequences for the Arab world and the world at large.

The resentment felt by the Egyptian army against Turkish rule was voiced by Ahmed Orabi. He was arrested for his complaints to the Khedive about ill-treatment of Egyptian officers in the army. Such was the resentment against the Khedive and Orabi's popularity, that his colleagues rescued him from jail by force on 9 September 1881. Orabi, along with his army supporters, led a march on horseback to the Khedive's palace. The Khedive, accompanied by the British Consul, met Orabi reluctantly and judging the temper of the times arrived at a temporary settlement with him. One of the demands of Orabi was the constitution of a parliament.

The Anglo-French authorities found a unique opportunity of sowing seeds of suspicion in the minds of the privileged Turkish minority in Egypt and in the mind of the Sultan of Turkey, whose nominee the Khedive was, with regard to this development. They conspired to frustrate Orabi in his designs. Ranged on one side were those with nationalist sentiments and on the other the Turkish and Anglo-British conspirators. Orabi expected an outbreak of hostility between his forces and the British and thus started fortifying Alexandria. On 11 July 1882, the British commander bombarded Alexandria. The French, however, disassociated themselves from the British in this open confrontation between Orabi and the British. A head-on collision between the two forces took place at Tel el Kabir in which Orabi was overwhelmed and the British consolidated their hold on Egypt. This was a sad day in the annals of Egyptian history because it was around this time, in 1885, that a revolution broke out in the Sudan, resulting in the end of Egyptian rule over the Sudan. A nominal Anglo-Egyptian administration was proclaimed for the Sudan in 1888, but the country was for all purposes under British control, and became free only in 1954.

The British, during their occupation of Egypt, treated the Egyptians poorly. Their accent on farming resulted in the initiation of a number of irrigation and canal development plans in Egypt. However, these measures were taken with an eye to holding the country from launching herself on the road to modernism and rapid industrialisation leading to economic self-sufficiency. The frustrations of those days, however, should be read as an unpleasant chapter in the history of the Egyptian revolution today. Egypt seems to have launched herself on the path of rapid industrialisation and large-scale reconstruction under the leadership of Sadat to make up for the lost decades.

THE RENAISSANCE

Historically, the three centuries of the Ottoman occupation of Egypt and Syria was a period of decay in these countries. However, the renaissance which followed in the late nineteenth century was an intellectual rather than a political one. Outstanding in this renaissance was the role of Egypt, for it was in Egypt that educated Arabs, while drawing upon traditionally cherished values, brought in a whole set of new ideas and the literature which was produced as a result was rich in modern political thought.

Contact with the West brought about a new wave of modernism on one hand and a dedication to traditional values on the other. The most powerful and progressive force was an amalgam of the two modernism of progress with spiritual and emancipatory patterns of thought. It promoted the growth of a resurgent nationalism as well as social realism. An analysis of the trends that such an awakening brought about has been discussed by the well-known modern Arabic poet and social realist, Salah Abdul Sabur in his book, *The Story of the Contemporary Egyptian Conscience* written in Arabic.

In the intellectual movement which took shape in the 1880s the role of Jamaluddin el Afghani was prominent. He tried to infuse new blood into Muslim society by injecting modernism in outlook and a scientific approach while preserving the basic spiritual and cultural values of Islam. His disciple, Sheikh Mohammed Abdu, gave concrete shape to his mentor's ideas and exercised a great influence on Muslim thought by stressing the need for intellectual reform and enlightenment. He considered such reform the pre-condition for political independence. They were the great pioneers of Egyptian nationalism.

The British occupation of Egypt in 1882, unlike the brief occupation by Napoleon in 1798, proved more prolonged than seemed probable at the time. The Egyptians banked on the French disapproval of British occupation, but unfortunately the two powers came to an understanding that the French possessions in northwest Africa would act as *quid pro quo* for the British occupation of Egypt. The colonialists knew the art of accommodating each other.

A nationalist party led by Mustafa Kamil arose in Egypt in 1907 which advocated self-help rather than dependence on the good intentions of the colonialists. Kamil believed that unless a nation developed its own potential and was able to win her independence by her own strength nothing worthwhile could be achieved. As against this the great social reformer Sheikh Mohammed Abdu was of the view that an intellectual enlightenment and renaissance could also lead to political freedom.

When the First World War broke out in 1914 the British declared Egypt a protectorate. The war situation acted as a brake to the national upsurge in Egypt, but no sooner was the war over when the nationalist movement once again raised its head. On 13 November 1918 Saad Zaghloul demanded complete independence for Egypt and the right to send an Egyptian representative to the Paris Peace Conference. As was to be expected, these demands were not even seriously listened to let alone granted.

Those were the days of awakening, unrest, agitation, and struggle, but the entire human and material potential of Egypt was then at the disposal of the British military authorities who had used coercion to recruit Egyptian labourers and farmers for service in Sinai, Iraq, Palestine, the Dardanelles and France during the First World War. The then Egyptian local government only acted as the instrument of the occupation power and implemented its dictates. The occupation authorities had also commandeered all fit animals in the country for transport at throwaway prices. Cattle and foodstuff were similarly requisitioned. The timber resources of Egypt had already been depleted and the local Government was forced to reduce the area of cultivation earmarked for cotton and to increase the areas of growing foodgrains to meet the logistic requirements of Britain and her Allies.

On 16 January 1916, Ismail Sirri Pasha, the War Minister, issued orders on behalf of the Council of Ministers to all on the reserve list to present themselves for military service except those who were serving the government in various capacities. This was done at the instance of the British Military Commander in Egypt who, in a letter to the Prime Minister, had demanded Egyptian manpower for the protection of the Suez Canal. Such a force could be formed from the reserve lists of the Egyptian army. A force of 12,000 was duly enrolled of conscripts from various parts of the country to defend the imperial interests. They were forced to work under unbearable and humiliating conditions. Impervious to their physical and mental needs the occupation authorities only succeeded in arousing their wrath and anger.

Their rebellious spirit exhibited itself on the dawn of 29 January 1916 when they staged a demonstration in front of the Abidin palace. Thousands of conscripts demonstrated against the British and against their inhuman conditions of service. The Prime Minister promised to look into their grievances but he failed to pacify them. Angry demonstrations were repeated on the following day resulting in firing and the use of force. As a result a number of them fell martyrs in the Abidin square. The incident roused nationalist sentiments everywhere.

On 10 October 1917 a new ministry was formed under the Prime Ministership of Hussein Rushdi Pasha, and Ismail Sirri Pasha became the War Minister. Within ten days of the formation of the Ministry Sirri Pasha issued a royal decree announcing conscription and collection of animal stock for war purposes. On 9 March 1918 the Ministry presided over by the Sultan decided that the Egyptian treasury would bear an expense of £3 million as compensation to be paid to Great Britain in recognition of her saving Egypt from foreign invasion of which half a million pounds were to meet the expenditure on the railways and the other £2.5 million for expenses incurred on account of the prosecution of war. On 11 November 1917 the First World War ended with the defeat of Germany and her allies. The Egyptians were now anxious to prevent the continued occupation of their land by the British after the conclusion of the war. Egypt had already paid dearly both in men and material during the war. Little did she realise that this was but the beginning of a phase in history when the imperialist forces would strengthen their foothold on her soil. They had not only taken control of political power in the country but had also established an effective control over the material resources of Egypt.

THE REVOLUTION OF 1919

The revolution which began in Egypt on 9 March 1919 affected not only the Arab countries but a number of countries of Asia to whom it became an example to follow. The Wafd party and its founder leader, Saad Zaghloul, made a great impression on the political scene. Saad Zaghloul represented not just one political party or a section of national opinion but the entire Egyptian people. Zaghloul did not merely represent the frustrations, the sufferings, and the economic burdens resulting from the First World War but an innate urge of the Egyptian people to be independent. The upsurge represented an organised revolution against colonialism.

At the end of the First World War, i.e., in 1918, Saad Zaghloul was a fifty-eight year old judge and had supported Orabi Pasha in his youth, for which he had been imprisoned. Under the influence of Sheikh Abdu he turned a reformer. It was on 13 November 1918 that Zaghloul, accompanied by a party deputation called on the British High Commissioner to demand the right of Egypt to send her representatives to the Paris Peace Conference at which he wanted to stake Egypt's claim to independence. This was refused. Saad was exiled and ultimately he died in 1927, with the leadership of the party passing on to Mustafa Nahas Pasha. The spirit of the 1919 Revolution never subsided and flared up intermittently. Britain was forced to open negotiations for a settlement on 28 February 1922 when Egypt was declared independent but with reservations. These reservations virtually granted the right to the British to locate troops on the soil of Egypt and wield effective power.

These were the circumstances in Egypt at the time of Sadat's birth on 25 December 1918. He was the child of the Revolution of 1919.

3

The Early Years and the War College

On his fifty-seventh birthday, i.e. 25 December 1975, President Sadat gave an interview on Cairo T.V. when he spoke of his early life, his beliefs, his hopes and fears, and of the story of Egypt and her revolution. Speaking of the New Year hopes for 1976 he listed the liberation of the Sinai as a sacred duty. Next, referring to the domestic scene, he announced his goal of achieving social security for every Egyptian national, no matter whether he lived in nearby towns or in far off villages. Striking a personal note he said that he would not like to see any Egyptian national suffer the privations which he had suffered in his early days, for Sadat was not born with a silver spoon in his mouth.

In the beginning of his interview Sadat spoke of his village Mit Abul Kom and described his life during the six years that he lived there. He spoke of his village teachers who taught him the Holy Qoran. The teacher of the Qoran was a hard task master and woe betide the defaulter. He spoke of his grandmother who, though lacking in formal education, had acquired great wisdom over the long years of her life. The President spoke of the 7,000 year old Egyptian civilisation and culture which the country had inherited, and which provided it with a strong base. He described how for the first time he absorbed impressions of British imperialism through the folk tales and ballads of Zahran Dinshewai and Adhem el Sharqavi. He spoke of his first experience of student demonstrations in Cairo protesting against the attempts of Ismail

Sidky imposing the constitution of the year 1930 to replace that of 1923. He said that although he was young, he was greatly moved and heartily participated in the students' strike which followed. The students entered the kitchen of the school, smashed up the crockery and then got on to the streets to upturn one of the trams and set it on fire. The President recalled that even at that age he did not quite believe in such methods for the furtherance of one's cause and that there should be better means of achieving one's end. Sadat spoke of the political disturbances which had gripped Egypt during the Second World War.

When asked if he had realised some of the hopes and aspirations of his youthful days, Sadat replied that one's hopes and aspirations also underwent an evolution with the passage of time. He had, nevertheless, realised quite a few of his ambitions. Egypt would never return to the rule of kings and monarchs. No longer would the son of an Egyptian labourer wear his father's mantle automatically for hereditary reasons nor would a watchman's son become a watchman for the same reason. Egypt had for the first time achieved equality of opportunity for every member of the society. Talking of his second aspiration, Sadat stated that he would like to realise for every Egyptian citizen complete social security against poverty, disease, incapacity and old age disabilities.

Sadat was in a reminiscent mood and spoke nostalgically of his early years. He had always managed to spend his birthdays back in his village whose soil had nourished him, except during the years he was being hounded by security officials. He spoke of his first teacher, Sheikh Abdul Hamid Issa, who had taught him the Qoran and who had died recently in Cairo at the age of eighty-six. Sadat made it a point to attend his funeral despite his exacting schedules, a key to his popularity with the masses and his identification with the sons of the soil.

His father had also learnt the Holy Book in his childhood and had studied enough to secure a primary school certificate. The learning of the Qoran by rote was one of the conditions for entry into the Al Azhar University. It was there that the knowledge of the Holy Qoran was perfected. Those days there were hardly any schools, particularly in the villages, but after the October 1952 revolution a new school was opened every third day. Sadat was nostalgic about his life in the village and spoke appreciatively of the many unwritten traditions which were followed in village life. If anyone died the entire village helped the bereaved family in performing the various rites. Unfortunately things had changed today. In fact, such was their brotherhood and consideration for one another in the past that if there was any occasion for merry-making during the period of bereavement of someone else in the village, one would go and obtain the permission of the affected family. People were respected for the values they held, and not according to whether they were rich or poor. Even in purely mundane matters such as the sowing of seeds and reaping of harvests there used to be collective participation. In fact the entire village acted as one family where everyone participated and helped according to his ability and capacity and everyone earned his bread by the sweat of his brow.

Sadat's father worked in the Sudan to earn his living. While he was away there, he used to leave his child with his grandmother. His father used to come home on his annual vacation which lasted three months. Sadat's grandmother played a great role in shaping Sadat. The grand old lady was not only a woman of great culture but also known for her stern character. She kept track of what was happening in the country at large, outside her immediate surroundings. She was the natural leader of the village and took an active part in solving its problems. The people of the village had got used to accepting her verdict as final whose implementation was to be immediate and binding on all parties. The grand old lady was extremely religious and had made it a practice to listen to the recitation and interpretation of the Holy Qoran. Her little grandson was her constant companion to whom she used to recite stories and folk tales. The young Anwar used to get into groups of village children every now and then to narrate to them the stories which he had heard from his grandmother.

This grandmother had a personal history. Before her marriage she had lived under the care of her uncle who was a colleague of the militant Egyptian leader Ahmed Orabi and had participated in fighting against the British occupation forces. Because of this she had imbibed the traditions of a simple faith and burning patriotism which were to leave strong imprints on the young mind of Sadat. The story of the struggle and sacrifices of Orabi and the struggle of the Egyptians against the British occupation forces, the story of the digging of the Suez Canal, the oppressive conditions under which the Egyptians worked, the inhuman treatment which they were accorded, the pangs of hunger and privation they suffered, and the story of the martyrs who fell in the Abidin square massacre were popular stories narrated to Sadat. These were the early years when his impressionable young mind absorbed the message of patriotism, struggle, and sacrifice. The seeds were sown in fertile soil and were to sprout and flourish one day. Sadat, even as a young child, was brought up in an atmosphere of strict religious discipline. Regular prayers and fasting had become a part of his routine. Such was his devotion and dedication in these matters that the people of his village had nicknamed him Sheikh Mohammed.

Detailed accounts are available of Sadat's early childhood. His earliest teacher was Sheikh Abdul Hamid Issa who taught a hundred and fifty children of the village. Sadat was known as Mohammed to his classmates and teachers. Sheikh Abdul Hamid has described Sadat as a calm and composed child. He was dutiful and obedient and preferred to sit in the front row in front of the teacher. He was an attentive listener, quick in understanding and assimilating. From an early age he had set his heart on an army career and went about it with all seriousness. Sadat maintained his contacts with his childhood colleagues such as Rafat, who later became a captain in the armed forces, and Paul Patrice, who became a teacher. According to them Sadat's parents decided to put him in the primary school, the only school in that area which was run by the Copts in the village of Tukh Delka at a distance of a kilometre from the village. They had passed out of the same school. It was decided in the case of Sadat that he should be put in the next higher class because in the preliminary test in Arabic and arithmetic he was found to be above average. According to Paul Patrice who continues to be a teacher in the same school, Sadat was a keen student of English, Arabic and arithmetic. He preferred walking to the school and was very fond of physical training. He maintained good relations with all the teachers and students alike. He was liked by people and he in turn liked people. Sadat maintains his interest in his native village to this day and never misses an opportunity to visit it if circumstances permit. On 9 October 1953 he visited the school and recorded the following message in the Visitors' Book: "God is Great and all glory, praise, and thanks are to God. The Almighty decreed that I should visit this place which trained me and brought me up and inspired in me a spirit of struggle in my life. In my opinion it is a place of worship and I travelled to it to reinforce myself once again with the power of faith and strength. I wish the members of the school all success. I would like to continue to serve this school so that I may be able to return a little of my gratitude to it. May God bless all and guide us on the correct path."[1]

In the year 1931 Sadat's father returned to Cairo from the Sudan and lived in a small house at Kobri el Kubbeh. The street was named the "Street of the Leader" which today faces the Kubbeh Palace. His father got Sadat admitted to a secondary school called 'Fuad I' in Abbasia. He agreed to pay the high tuition fees prescribed in those days for that school. The President, while speaking of this period of his life, stated that his father was not in a position to bear the expenses of both his and his brother's education and was therefore obliged to select one of them for better education. He recalled that his entry into the secondary school was, therefore, a matter of pure chance. One of his classmates, Syed Ahmed Shafiq Haseeb, who continued as his colleague later in the War College says of this period:

We were a generation older than our physical ages. We were serious and rough. We lived our boyhood days listening to the story of the revolution which broke out in the year 1919 and how a large number of people fell martyrs. We heard of the trials which were conducted by the British military occupation authorities; 51 of those sent up for trial were guillotined. Several thousands were arrested and lashed publicly in the cities of Cairo, Assiut, Al Wasti, Al Minia, Rashid, Qalyub, Beni Suef and Alexandria. The story of these trials fired our imagination and created in us an intense hatred of imperialism and its henchmen, the Pashas and their minions. It was, therefore, not surprising that the students of the secondary school spent a good deal of time reflecting on the national movement. They were fully concerned with group action against British occupation in the thirties. Sadat was one of us and yet he was different from us in as much as the national movement seemed to occupy his whole attention. He made no secret of his burning hatred of the forces which had occupied our country. He dis-

---

[1]*Anwar el Sadat*, (Arabic), Hamdi Lutfi, Darul Maarif, Cairo, 1972, p. 33.

played a powerful personality in influencing the students around him and conveying to them some of his own burning enthusiasm. In his own way he tried to instil a spirit of freedom and independence in his contacts with his colleagues at school. He spent five years in the secondary school in which he established an intimate and personal contact with the people and the surroundings. He was all praise for the Egyptian army and was highly appreciative of Ahmed Orabi Pasha and his colleagues. It almost became his daily routine to talk about Orabi Pasha and write out placards highlighting the nationalist slogans of Orabi. Orabi's inspiration played no mean role in his decision to enter the War College. He was a dreamer and nursed many ambitions, the foremost being to serve a quit notice on the British imperialist forces occupying the soil of his native land.[2]

The British were initially on guard from the Egyptian army rank and file but later they permitted them to join the War College. There was a plan behind it. The British were laying the basis for the armed forces of a country which they were going to colonise. By opening the gates of the War College to the sons of the soil, they aimed at using the Egyptian army to protect their imperialist interests in North Africa. Just as the British planned to utilise the youth of the Egyptian army in the furtherance of their own interests, it was paradoxical that the generation which was born in the wake of the 1919 revolution was similarly thinking in terms of utilising the opportunity of their getting into the army to gain their national objectives. The War College turned out a number of youthful leaders fired with the zeal of revolution, and the class which graduated in February 1938 was notable for the prominent part it played in the liberation of the country. It was ultimately the Free Officers of the Egyptian armed forces who were able to consummate the revolution. Despite the regimented training they received from military instructors at the College, their sense of patriotism and dedication to their cause remained undimmed. They were prepared to pay any price to achieve their goal. No sacrifice was considered by them too great in this cause.

Though the army assured a social status as well as a certain

---

[2]Hamdi Lutfi, *op. cit.*

The Early Years and the War College

amount of economic independence in the prevailing unemployment and economic depression, Sadat was basically a nationalist, a crusading politician rather than a professional soldier. He was a politician who had adopted the uniform rather than the other way round. Egypt partly needed both a national revolution as well as a social revolution and both Nasser and Sadat were convinced that such a broad united platform which could bring about such a revolution in that setting was the army. The army was the weapon which the Egyptian king wielded to keep his people under subjugation and once the army was taken control of, the king would be deprived of his trump card.

In October 1935 the biggest batch of Egyptian youth consisting of 40 cadets entered the War College and on 6 October 1936, the War College announced acceptance of a new term. This was the batch to which Gamal Abdel Nasser, Anwar el Sadat, the late Gen Abdul Munim Riad, and Hussein el Shafei belonged. Nasser had initially been rejected on the ground that he had participated in an anti-British demonstration during which he was injured and his photograph, showing him injured, had appeared in a local newspaper. Nasser, therefore, turned to the Law College for a while but would not give up and soon returned to the War College through his persistent efforts and joined it on 17 March 1937.

The batch which entered the War College on 6 October 1936 passed out in February 1938. This batch was not only fired with a burning sense of patriotism but was bound by the deep comradeship which existed between its various members which survived the onslaughts of time and events. According to the majority of colleagues who passed out of the War College that year, those who distinguished themselves in understanding the political currents and cross-currents sweeping the country and who set the pattern for patriotic thinking and action were Nasser and Sadat. Their maturity of judgement and understanding of historical forces far outweighed the relative immaturity of their young age. The British Commander of the War College was a stickler for detail, particularly with those cadets about whom he wanted to have every possible detail. In the beginning Sadat was commissioned into infantry but later he was transferred to the Signal Corps. During the Second World War the Egyptian officers and troops were charged with the task of protecting the Canal

Zone. One complete batch of officers passing out was sent to the war front in Palestine.

Nasser's relationship with Sadat, a very colourful and buoyant personality, was based on Sadat's appreciation of Nasser's character, his burning patriotism and his selflessness. Anwar el Sadat has described how, if the group of Young Officers at Mankabad tried to sidetrack the main issue of freedom-fight and indulged in light-hearted gossip, Nasser used to bring them back on to the rails. Nasser was always serious and totally dedicated to the task he had set for himself.

In September 1938 the legendary General Aziz el Masry was the Chief of Staff of the Egyptian armed forces, and general Wilson the Commander of the British forces in the Middle East. General Masry was to figure prominently in Sadat's early career. Masry was not only a competent general but also a shrewd student of political affairs. A reported piece of conversation between General Masry and General Wilson shows the professional competence of the former. The Egyptian general was discussing the merits of concentrating the British forces in Mersa Matruh. General Wilson was of the opinion that any Italian advance from the West or any advance by any other force from Libya would be exposed to attack by defences if located in Mersa Matruh. General Masry disagreed and pointed to the valley south of Mersa Matruh, which was away from the gun range of Mersa Matruh by four kilometres and opined that any Italian advance south of this point through the valley would not only be immune to any bombardment from Mersa Matruh but would also expose Mersa Matruh to an outflanking movement without a shot being fired, a fact borne out by subsequent developments. General Masry is reported to have recommended defences around Alamein.

Sadat was fond of General Masry, and said about him:

The General was a small, slight man with a light complexion and grey eyes. Despite his advanced age he had tremendous energy and fire. He combined the qualities of a soldier with those of a diplomat, controlling a passionate temperament with a will of iron.

He had achieved brilliant success during the Balkan War of 1912-1914 and again in Libya where he fought with the Turkish army against the Italians. He was receptive to modern ideas, having travelled in France, England and Germany. His experience, his patriotism and his past record were such as to arouse the suspicion of the British and to make his services eminently valuable to the revolutionary movement."[3]

---

[3]*Revolt on the Nile*, Anwar el Sadat, Allan Wingate Ltd., London, 1957, p. 31.

4

The Free Officers Take the Plunge

To imagine that the Revolution of 1919 suddenly erupted and as swiftly subsided in Egypt would be to misread history and misjudge the Egyptian temper. The Egyptian struggle continued after that and in a sense persisted till the bitter end—with varying degrees of intensity until the final act of liberation. These long years of struggle were interspersed with acts of political violence such as the murder of the Sirdar of the Sudan, Sir Lee Stack, on 19 November 1924. The British government reacted to this murder harshly by imposing an indemnity of £500,000, ordering forced withdrawal of all Egyptian forces from the Sudan and inflicting several other punitive measures.[1]

The Wafd party had, therefore, established its popularity with the masses as it gave expression to the spirit of national upsurge which in turn was resented by King Fuad. The King dissolved the Egyptian Parliament and established an autocratic regime with British support. The British support to King Fuad was aimed at suppressing the popularity of the Wafd party. King Fuad played havoc with ministries. Several ministries were constituted and dissolved without much ceremony and this sordid drama continued until the death of King Fuad in April 1936.

Mustafa Nahas Pasha, who had become Prime Minister in May 1936, visited London in August the same year and nego-

---
[1] *The Times* (London), 24 November 1924.

tiated the Anglo-Egyptian Treaty of 1936. The Treaty, though formally terminating the status of Egypt as a British protectorate, nevertheless required her to participate in her anticipated war effort. The agreement was to last 20 years and permitted Britain to locate 10,000 troops and 40 pilots in the Canal zone. The Agreement also provided that the parties could revise it after a period of 10 years. Under the terms, a British Military Mission was to advise the Egyptian army in all military matters. The Agreement was hailed at that time as a partial victory for the Wafd Party but those who looked beyond the nose saw in it sinister designs.

The acceptance of the 1936 Treaty by the Egyptian leaders came as a disillusionment to young and free minds like those of Nasser and Sadat who, though no more than young men, were conscious of the political currents and cross-currents which were sweeping the country. The Treaty was a retrograde step in Nasser's view. In all vital matters, such as the control of the Sudan, the defence of the Canal zone or the control of the Egyptian army, Britain was the ultimate arbiter. The rise of Italian fascism, its defiance of the League of Nations and its aggression on close-by Abyssinia on the one hand and British manoeuvres on the other had put Egypt between the devil and the deep sea. The presence of the British troops in the Canal zone was even an act of provocation for the Axis powers and the vital struggle for communication lines had already been joined. The war clouds were gathering fast. The Italians had not only aggressed against Abyssinia, they had let loose a reign of terror in Libya, and Egypt, even in her unenviable position, was not impervious to the fate of a sister Arab country. She, however, did not have much choice.

A group of young officers used to meet in the garrison of Mankabad in 1938 around a camp fire, burning with the zeal of freedom and independence for their country. They wanted to rid the country of imperialism, monarchy, and feudalism through a revolution. Nasser and Sadat were the leading lights of this movement. They were clear about what they wanted and set about earnestly to achieve what they wanted. War clouds were forming on the horizon. Somehow, the uncertainties of the war situation, they thought, would give them an opportunity to strike. The idea crystallised in 1939 in the shape of a secret revolutionary society whose members were dedicated to liberating their country. The stage for revolution was set. The Revolutionary Command Council, in fact, was a development of the Society of Free Officers. The society initially consisted of ten officers of which Nasser was the President and the other members were Abdul Hakim Amer, Kamaluddin Hussein, Salah Salem, Khalid Mohiuddin, and Anwar el Sadat. There were four officers from the Air Force—Gamal Salem, Hasan Ibrahim, Abdul Latif Baghdadi, and Abdul Muneim Abdul Raouf.

Sadat has maintained copious diaries in which he has recorded his impressions of the first days of the meetings of the revolutionaries after they passed out of the War College. He used to commit these proceedings to writing and distribute them among the army units. In one of these recordings Sadat has this to say: "This revolution started naturally and its growth was also natural. It was because at all stages it represented a natural reaction between the conscience of the army of Egypt and the conscience of its revolutionary people."

The unity of purpose and comradeship that existed between the officers had obliterated all ideas of differences in age, rank or position. They were bound by a common dedication to the cause. Nasser had a knack of expressing the most complicated things in a simple and direct manner. Even though one knew all about the nature of British imperialism and the political and other troubles which Egypt was having at that time, Nasser's short epigrammatic sentences seemed to hit the nail on the head. Those were the initial stages when the ideological background of the Free Officers received its initial baptism. Like the rays of the sun which spread in all directions, the centre of this radiation appeared to be the Free Officers supported by the vast mass of the people.

Sadat says the following about the situation in Egypt at the time of the outbreak of the Second World War:

The social structure of Egypt on the eve of the Second World War can be compared to that of France before the revolution of 1789. At the top, King Farouk and his family, the dynasty of Muhammad Ali, disposed of roughly one-fourth of the national income. This Albanian royal house shallowly rooted in national sentiment, had usurped its powers in the 19th century. The dynasty wore itself out by its excesses....

In 1939, two million Egyptian tenant farmers were so poor

The Free Officers Take the Plunge 35

that they did not even own simple tools to till their fields. The peasant proletariat of Egypt was an amorphous, passive, dumb mass of people whose chief preoccupation was survival. . . .

In 1939 the sky clouded over, the storm burst. The Second World War scattered our revolutionary group to the four winds. Gamal Abdel Nasser was sent to the Sudan, the country artificially separated from Egypt by a line drawn across the map by the British. . . .

Sudan, at this time, was a land of exile for army officers in disfavour. In fact, in an area bigger than Europe, almost anywhere outside Cairo and Alexandria was a place of exile for people who had ceased to discharge their function as 'satisfactory' servants of the state . . . .

Lt Nasser was calm and deep, always master of his emotions. Small setbacks did not disturb him but they upset Abdul Hakim who was impulsive and unpredictable.

The British dominated the country. They held Egypt in a net of political and military obligations from which she could not free herself. In theory Egypt's sovereignty had been restored by the treaty of 26 August 1936. In fact the country remained in bondage. Mixed up in a burning conflict in which we had no interest, Egypt became nothing more than a satellite of the British empire.[2]

General Masry, the Egyptian Chief of Staff who was sympathetic to the Free Officers, was fond of collecting the brighter officers around him and holding weekly tête-à-têtes every Wednesday when he discussed strategic, tactical, and administrative matters concerning the army. One of the officers of those days, Hussein Mutawalli, has stated that during these weekly meetings he could remember Sadat as a very serious and enthusiastic participant in discussions. It was on the initiative of General Masry that new workshops and war factories were established in Egypt for the first time and one of the first Egyptian armoured cars was produced under his inspiration. The proposals of General Masry for the reorganisation and re-fitment of the Egyptian army raised a hornet's nest. The British authorities almost considered it treasonable and he fell foul of the court. During those days the Free Officers used to bring out and distribute their news bulletins

[2] *Revolt on the Nile, op. cit.*

and other instructions secretly through various means. Sometimes these used to be circulated through official channels along with other official mail and sometimes by ordinary post. This literature was planted sometimes in offices, bedrooms, windows, almirahs and various files. The Free Officers and the members of the Revolutionary Command Council in the forefront used to watch the reaction of the recipients of these bulletins. Some of them used to read them and preserve them so that they could show them to others. Some used to rush to the Royal Intelligence Services as informers and agents and some used to read them and destroy them without leaving a trace. They had hardly dealt with one when they had the next one in hand. The Free Officers were thus able to have a proper assessment of the potential of various officers, their inclinations, and the strength of their nationalist sentiment.

General Masry had served as the tutor of King Farouk in 1936. In one of the early meetings which Sadat had with General Masry, he described the futile attempts made by him to equip King Farouk with the type of education which would enable him to discharge his royal functions adequately but in vain.

The early relationship between Sadat and General Masry was to bring them together in a series of attempts for the establishment of direct contact between General Masry and the Germans. A series of encounters have been described by Sadat in his book *Revolt on the Nile*, largely about escapades for smuggling General Masry out of Egypt to Germany so that detailed plans could be laid for getting rid of the British. The very first attempt was to get him out of the country in a German submarine from Lake Borolos near the Canal zone. The plan did not materialise. The next attempt was to use a disused airfield from where a German air force plane would pick up General Masry and his companions. Unfortunately, the airfield was a bad choice because huge British supply dumps were located near it. This plan also proved abortive. Another attempt was made when a plane landed at an agreed rendezvous but unfortunately the General could not reach the venue in time as his car broke down. Finally the General attempted to fly away in an Egyptian military aircraft but unluckily the aircraft hit a post and the occupants were injured.

General Masry was by any standards a patriot who was dedicated to his country as well as to his profession. Sadat as a young officer under him speaks appreciatively of the great qualities of head and heart displayed by Masry. Sadat recalled many inspiring talks Masry gave lamenting the fact that such an important country as Egypt, located in such a strategic area and with a glorious past should be treated in such a cavalier fashion by the occupying power. Referring to the young officers, Masry said that they were the only hope for Egypt. Referring to the feeling among the young officers that they were still young and inexperienced, Sadat recalled Masry's comment that Napoleon was only twenty-seven when helped his country and his army in expeditions. He wanted young officers to learn the lesson of self-reliance and self-confidence.

On 10 June 1940, when Italy declared war she had more than 200,000 troops in Libya and about 80,000 troops on the Egyptian borders and the Libyan desert. The Allied troops did not number more than 50,000. Ali Maher, who was the Egyptian Prime Minister at that time, was under pressure by the British authorities to enter the war formally but he played for time. On 22 June 1940, Ali Maher was removed from office and General Aziz el Masry, the Egyptian Chief of Staff, was dismissed in August 1940 for his alleged pro-Axis sympathies. It was at this stage that while Sadat was in touch with Nasser and the Free Officers on the one hand, he was also in touch with the domestic front on the other. On the domestic front he wanted to enlist the support of the Muslim Brotherhood, while his foreign policy was to establish some contact with the Germans so that this twin move would pave the way for the ejection of the British occupation forces. Sadat would have us believe that for both these actions he had the mandate from the Revolutionary Command Council.

The year 1940 was a bad period for Britain and France. Marshal Petain had capitulated to the Nazis. The French Commanders in the Middle East and Africa had, after a period of hesitation, decided not to revolt against Petain. Between 1940 and 1942 the Axis powers scored a series of triumphs in North Africa. The German war hero Rommel had proved his mettle on the sandy battle fields of North Africa. Nasser and Sadat were so resentful of the British occupation of their country that they thought the only way out was for an Axis victory in that part of the world and an Allied defeat. They hoped that by this means Egypt would be rid of British occupation and in this they would even want to establish secret contact with the Germans to facilitate the ouster of the British. Two German officers dressed as British officers came to the Allied lines in 1942 with forged currency notes worth £50,000. These two officers established a spy nest in a houseboat on the Nile. Sadat was implicated in this and was arrested. He escaped from prison and re-established his contacts with Nasser.

On the war front, as the British faced hard times, they tightened their grip on Egypt. Sadat says of this phase:

> Encouraged by the isolation of the British in the Middle East, Mussolini launched an offensive from Libya....
>
> On September 14 the Italians occupied Sollum. On the 17th they took Sidi Barrani, 60 miles inside Egyptian territory. Graziani placed his infantry about 25 miles east of Sidi Barrani. Then he hesitated. The British, worn out, had nothing with which to oppose him. But Graziani waited and he gave the British time to get their second wind, regroup and bring reinforcements....
>
> Churchill decided that Egypt must be completely subordinated to the British war machine, using whatever degree of intimidation proved necessary. Churchill began by neutralising the Egyptian army. Through the British military authorities in the Middle East, he ordered the Egyptian High Command to disarm and immediately withdraw all Egyptian forces from Mersa Matruh in the Western Desert.[3]

When the Italian forces started advancing towards Mersa Matruh in September 1940 the Egyptian units located along the line acquitted themselves well, until an order was issued by the then Egyptian government headed by Ali Maher Pasha that they should adopt a neutral attitude in the fighting by rival forces. This order came as a big surprise to the British authorities and to the British Commander of the Middle Eastern forces. The British at this time ordered that the equipment and weapons loaned to the Egyptian army should be returned to them, particularly the heavier equipment. The Egyptian army was asked to return to Cairo leaving their weapons and equipment behind.

The Egyptian army authorities, however, refused to pocket this insult and returned to Cairo with their complete weapons and

---

[3]*Revolt on the Nile, op. cit.*

The Free Officers Take the Plunge 39

equipment. The British behaviour was outrageous in the extreme. Their forces were deployed in front of Mersa Matruh as a precautionary measure lest the Egyptian troops blew up the arms and ammunition dumps located there, if they were forced to surrender their weapons before returning to Cairo. Due to the exigencies of service the leading lights of the Free Officers Movement were posted to distant places during the war years, yet the bond between them remained steady. Sometimes, for example, Nasser would be away for two years at a time, as between December 1939 and December 1941 when he was posted to the Sudan. Yet his silent guiding spirit seemed to remain behind with those who were to implement his ideas.

The early days of 1940 were eventful, particularly the battle field around Mersa Matruh. The Officers were dispersed in the Western desert, in the Sudan, and all over Egypt. Nasser was moved from Mankabad to Alamein, where he spent four months, then to Abi Zabal and to the Sudan. These movements provided Nasser with another opportunity of creating cadres of like-minded persons. Each one in the Free Officer's group was similarly inclined and conducted himself in a like manner. Though the general feeling was clear yet they were not sure of what was to be done under the circumstances. The aim was clear enough, i. e. to rid the country of the British occupation. There was realisation of the fact that during the pendency of the war this was not possible. The British had complete control over all vital installations, bases and means of communication. The irony of the situation was that the Egyptian army was also supposed to be fighting alongside the British to protect imperial interests.

Sadat, as the world came to know, was together with Nasser, the co-architect of the revolution of 23 July 1952. Sadat was well known for at least ten years before the revolution as being foremost among its planners. None harboured any doubts about his being a dedicated officer, ready to sacrifice his all in the cause of the country's freedom. He was in love with Egypt and had suffered the tyranny of the British authorities, fell foul of them, and faced persecution at the hands of King Farouk. He bore calamities with a smile and maintained his equanimity under all circumstances, even in prison. He was adept at jumping prison walls and in underground operations without his patriotic fervour showing any signs of abating. He was an ideal officer in his time and set an example both to his seniors and his juniors, and established a reputation for being straightforward and true to his word. His exuberance sometimes led to certain dangerous situations, and as stated by Sadat himself, Nasser's wisdom used to act as a brake on hasty adventurism. It was during this period that Sadat's qualities shone.

Campaign analyses in the past have shown that armed forces personnel, who are generally religious-minded and cherish spiritual values function better on the battle-field than those who do not cherish such values. It is not in the narrow sense that religion has any value, but in being truly religious, i. e. dedication to certain principles of behaviour and conduct, a certain pride in oneself, a belief in a cause, loyalty to colleagues, and an instant readiness to offer any sacrifice cheerfully and willingly for a cause. In this respect Sadat lived his life dangerously and cheerfully hazarded it, equipped with full faith in his mission and his cause.

Soon after he passed out of the War College, when he was hardly twenty-one, he sought the assistance of some of his colleagues to build a small mosque for the Signal Corps to which he belonged. He was punctual in his daily prayers even at that time, an act which inspired some very senior commanders to follow his example. In the higher rungs of the ladder there were two personalities who held out any hope for the Free Officers—Ali Maher, the Prime Minister who had achieved fame by his call for Egyptian neutrality in war, and General Masry. The young officers pinned their hopes on obtaining their support. They tried to get in touch with Ali Maher but failed for various reasons. However, they were a little more successful with Masry.

In conception and organisation, the Free Officers movement had no clearcut plans. These were developed as a result of the exigencies of the situation and the various trials and experiments which were conducted. The revolutionary group was divided into two sections, the military and the civil section. The former was headed by Nasser himself whereas Sadat headed the latter. Later, an administrative section was conceived by Nasser.

Sadat was chiefly responsible for the establishment of contact between the German High Command and the Egyptian Free Officers. Rommel sent two agents to Cairo in 1942 who contacted Sadat through a Major Hasan Izzat. One of the two agents, Hans Appler, who had changed his name to Hussein Thaffar, had a German mother and Egyptian father and was fluent in Arabic. The two German spies used to don British uniforms and move about in the Siwa Oases in a car fixed with a British number plate. Their high-living, immature behaviour, and lavish spending of counterfeit currency ultimately landed them in trouble. They were arrested by British intelligence and nothing much came out of the whole exercise.

Sadat was arrested for complicity, was tried by a special court consisting of two British officers and an Egyptian officer, and was sentenced on 8 October 1942 to be cashiered and committed to a detention camp. He was detained at a village about 4 kilometres south of Minia and later shifted to another detention centre where he fell sick. He was transferred to a hospital in Qasr el Aini where he established contact with a secret network of helpers and sympathisers. That provided an opportunity to Sadat to escape from detention. After the escape he adopted the name of Al Haaj Mohammed Nuruddin and functioned as a contractor and transport agent for some time. He also established contacts, while doing these odd jobs, with some of his colleagues. These days were strenuous both physically and mentally for Sadat. Chased by the security services, he spent several anxious years and faced hard times. He was separated from his family and was hounded all the time. Sadat, recounting those days, mentions of his immense satisfaction when he heard through one of his colleagues that the revolutionary cadre had arranged to deliver £10 per month to his family for maintenance. This was a silver lining in the otherwise dark clouds gathering around his personal life and in the national affairs of the time. His house was constantly under observation and the security police conducted raids on it frequently. Sadat remembers with a chuckle the hide and seek game he played with them and the experience he gained of their methods.

Despite his young age Sadat was prone to treating the men in his unit in a fatherly fashion and used to address many of them as his sons, a characteristic which has survived to this day. He made it a point to participate with them in feasts and on other social occasions. He discouraged officers from wearing trinkets such as gold rings etc. He was particularly solicitous of the troops' welfare and believed in being fair, firm, and friendly without being abusive or overbearing. An interesting sidelight on Sadat's personality is thrown by an incident which occurred immediately before the outbreak of the revolution. He had information of impending action and wanted to be at a particular place at a time appointed for him. He was holding charge of the cash box of his unit and he meticulously handed over every penny of it to his second-in-command, took a train secretly, and reached Cairo after sunset on 22 July 1952. The men of his unit next heard his voice over the radio.

The revolution which was plotted in the Officers' Club was not mere revenge on the King or his agents, but had the noble purpose of launching Egypt on a new and revolutionary path with a modern and solid foundation. It was not meant to be an action by a group of officers to capture power or wreak vengeance but a well-studied and patriotic move to regain for Egypt the eminent position she deserved. The movement was, therefore, a singularly united one, in which the armed forces and the masses marched together to herald a new era in Egypt's history.

The period in which Sadat's revolutionary activities blossomed forth was also marked by an adverse war situation in the Western desert for the Allies against the relentless advance of Rommel, the "desert fox." The British had evacuated Bengazi after an unsuccessful battle in Januray 1942. The Germans had surrounded Tobruk. On 26 May 1942 the Germans launched their attack against the British Eighth Army commanded by General Ritchie. In these battles the Germans had an upper hand and they occupied Bir Hakim south-west of Tobruk as a result of which the British withdrew from the south of Tobruk in the middle of June 1942.

21 June 1942 witnessed the fall of Tobruk in which 3,000 British troops were taken prisoners. The Allies feared that the Germans would advance up to Alexandria and Cairo without much resistance. At the end of June 1942, the British had evacuated Mersa Matruh and Fuka and had decided on firming in around the Qattara depression which presented a bottleneck defensive position. The battle between the contending forces began on 1 July 1942 and lasted seven days and for the first time the British forces stood their ground.

Rommel returned to his offensive in August and September 1942. The British plan provided for withdrawal from Alamein all along the road between Alexandria and Cairo. The events bore out General Masry's tactical appreciation as mentioned earlier. Alamein seemed to work. Nevertheless, the British were apprehensive of their rear lines of withdrawal. This led to the rounding up of inconvenient elements in the Egyptian officer ranks. Sadat was the target and was isolated from the army on grounds of his complicity in undesirable activities. Nasser was in Sudan when Sadat made his attempt to establish contact with the Germans. Nasser returned from the Sudan and joined the Military Academy as an instructor only on 7 February 1943 and re-established contact with Sadat. By now the war situation had altered in favour of the Allies and the threat to the Middle East was over

5

Dawn of Revolution

The open challenge posed by Arab nationalism in general and Egyptian nationalism in particular sent a wave of alarm in Anglo-U. S. circles. They did not take long to react and the result was the creation of the state of Israel, which shocked the Arab world but provided the corrupt monarchy of Egypt an opportunity to kill two birds with one stone. They thought this was a good opportunity to get rid of the army and a few of its officers who they thought were creating trouble for them. With indifferent and outdated weapons and without any preparation for war these officers were sent to the Palestinian front with the full knowledge that they were exposed to an unequal fight where they had no chance of winning against the well-equipped and well-trained Israeli forces.

Secondly, by posing to be taking a lead in fighting Israel with their army, the corrupt royal regime wished to win kudos for this very "patriotic act." Once again an opportunity offered itself for the innate qualities of the Egyptian soldiery to manifest itself as in the days of Muhammed Ali. Though the Egyptian troops were thrown into a hopeless situation they showed extraordinary grit. An Egyptian garrison faced a siege at Falouga for four months under the young Gamal Abdel Nasser. Nasser himself was seriously wounded. Lying bleeding on the battlefield Nasser's thoughts wandered to the "greed, intrigue, and passion" which were playing havoc with the destiny of Egypt and with the destiny of the

Arabs as a whole. Thus Falouga became the first nail in the coffiin of the Farooqian monarchy.

The Palestinian problem gave a special edget o the Egyptian revolution. Never before had an entire people been uprooted and despatched to wherever they could find a place under the skies. Nevertheless, the West needed a military post in the heartland of the Arab world so that it could play off the progressives against the status qoist regimes there. According to the documents presented by the Palestinian spokesman Al Haj Amin el Hussaini, the Jews of Palestine did not own more than 7 per cent of the total land of Palestine when the British mandate ended on 15 May 1948. It would even be correct to say that the Zionists saw the future of the Palestinians even more clearly than the Palestinians and the Arabs themselves. Between the years 1936 and 1939, 184 Palestinians were hanged on charges of possessing weapons and ammunition. General Maitland Wilson, who was the British Commander-in-Chief of Egypt, said once that 500 Arab Palestinians were conducting guerrilla warfare against the British in such a way that it was not possible for a complete British division consisting of about 15,000 troops to contain them. The movement was local and regional and limited in scope and design.

One of the basic mistakes which the Arabs made in the beginning was not to look at the Palestinian problem as an integral part of a world-wide strategy. They looked at it in narrow regional terms. The Zionists on the other hand had a long-term plan up their sleeves. In 1943 the Zionists established a Jewish Corps to participate in the Second World War. This was done to create a trained reserve of committed Zionists and to impress upon the Allies that at the time of their need they had fought for them and were thus entitled to their support in return. In the Arab fold this was not realised until at a very late stage. Both at the end of the First World War and that of the Second, the Zionists maintained an intimate contact with world powers trying to obtain the maximum possible moral and material assistance. The Arabs ignored world powers, and viewed the situation in a narrow perspective. Israel was able to obtain almost immediate recognition by the USA, the Soviet Union, and Britain whereas the Arab viewpoint went by default. The United States recognised Israel within a few minutes of its formation, and the Soviet Union followed suit, whereas the Arab countries were beset with domestic problems and lacked even a comprehensive understanding of the issues involved. Even their support to the Palestinian cause remained largely at the verbal level.

Sadat was re-arrested in 1946 and released in 1948, the year of the birth of Israel. He engaged himself in private business in 1949 but managed to return to the armed forces in 1950. His friendship with Nasser, which had been interrupted since 1940 when the latter went to the Sudan, was resumed once again.

Nasser had assumed full control of the Free Officers' Movement in 1942 and retained it until the revolution was staged in July 1952. He was the motive power behind the organisation from 1942 to 1948 when Sadat was mostly in prison and concentration camps. On Sadat's return to the army in 1950 Nasser and Abdul Hakim Amer were the first colleagues to contact him. They visited Sadat at his Manial home and helped him with his promotion examination.

Nasser had formed a command organisation, the Free Officers' Constituent Body, and had selected those colleagues for its membership who had fought with him in the Palestinian war. Sadat was included in it due to his political record. The relationship between Nasser and Sadat was of an abiding nature and remained an intimate one till the very end.

It was agreed by the Revolutionary leaders on 8 October 1951 that the Anglo-Egyptian Treaty signed on 26 August 1936 should cease to have effect from then on and that the British should no longer enjoy any special privileges, concessions, and other facilities which they had enjoyed in Egypt in matters of wireless transmission, transport, customs, and logistic assistance to the armed forces. Egyptian workers, railwaymen and others refused to transport British soldiers and their supplies from Port Said and other ports which were intended to reinforce their Canal Zone deployment. On 13 October 1951 a British ship arrived at Port Said with 3,000 officers and soldiers. On landing they discovered that there was no further train service to convey them to their respective camps. They eventually went by road and were sabotaged and a number of lives were lost. The loss to the British in the course of a week's operations against them in the Canal Zone cost them about £2 million. A large number of Egyptians working in British camps sympathised with the commandos and left their posts of duty disregarding the loss of pay and nearly paralysed the services in deference to the call for national solidarity against British occupation.

On 16 October 1951 an open demonstration was staged in Ismailia against the British mounted patrols in the Canal Zone and in this direct confrontation several lives were lost on both sides. The British were forced to obtain their supplies not through local sources but from outside by means of aircrafts and ships. The only bridge, the Firdan bridge, which connected the railway communications between the Sinai peninsula and the rest of Egypt over the Canal became a special point of control. This was the only means by which the Egyptian forces camping in Al Arish, Gaza, and the Sinai peninsula could be approached, and the British attempt was to isolate the Egyptian people from their armed forces.

Despite this temporary breach in the means of physical communication between the Egyptian troops in the Sinai and those west of the Canal, Nasser and Sadat organised resistance by all available means. Many blocks of houses had machine-guns mounted on them to fire on reinforcements headed for British camps. The Free Officers wanted to give an organisational base to the spirit of resistance which was crystallising in Egypt, and yet the then Egyptian government issued orders at the end of November 1951 that no organisation or individual should form resistance battalions or collect funds or carry out training. The Government Order said that any such action would lie within the competence of the Government itself.

The Canal Zone operations, nevertheless, continued with various degrees of intensity, particularly on 17 and 18 November 1951 in which the police also joined the resistance squads. In a single engagement 13 Egyptians and 5 British officers were killed and hundreds injured. The Commander of the British forces, General Erskine, sent peace-feelers to restore calm in the Canal Zone. A temporary agreement was arrived at enabling the British families to be evacuated from Ismailia and other Canal towns. In Suez, resistance was launched in an organised manner on 3 December 1951 when the British troops mounted on armoured cars resorted to indiscriminate firing. Another serious engagement lasting forty-eight hours took place on 3 and 4 January 1952 in which 25 tanks and more than 600 British troops participated. A precarious ceasefire was arranged on 4 January 1952. While the embers were still bright in port Suez, resistance broke out in the Abu Suweir area of Ismailia. A battalion of British paratroopers were landed in the area and they resorted to reprisals against the civil population of Ismailia. According to independent observers and international reporting of events during those days, the Egyptian resistance groups as well as the civil population rose to great heights of valour and courageous functioning against the organised forces of the British infantry, paratroopers and mounted troops.

It would be interesting to recall the opinion which Sadat's seniors had of him since he started his career in the armed forces. The first ever report was submitted on him covering the period 2 November 1939 to April 1940. The report mentions, apart from his excellent physical condition, his sense of self-respect and respect for his seniors. His devotion to duty and diligence find a mention. He was described as calm and collected, displaying technical and professional competence which won for him the respect of his colleagues and the appreciation of his senior commanders. The consistently good reports which he obtained speak of his good behaviour and exemplary conduct, his sense of discipline and technical proficiency. In the report which was submitted in April 1952, i.e. three months before the famous revolution was staged, Sadat was described as one with a strong personality, honest and devoted and popular among his subordinates.

Sadat has made a few pertinent observations which are a key to his personality and his political philosophy. He wrote:

> In every revolution there are two phases. First, man leads the revolution, then the revolution leads men.... I was ordered by the Revolutionary Committee to get in touch with two of the dominating figures on the Egyptian political scene: Sheikh Hassan el Banna, the Supreme Guide of the Muslim Brotherhood and General Aziz el Masry, Chief of Staff of the Army. The Muslim Brotherhood was founded by Hassan el Banna in Ismailia in 1930. Its ostensible aim was the moral perfection of the individual but its underlying aim was the reorganisation of society in an ideal plane. Originally the Brotherhood had no political objective; it simply expressed the wave of moral regeneration which was transforming Egypt. The austere virtues of the Supreme Guide contrasted with the basement of the people in high authority in the State. His influence on the masses grew.

President Fakhruddin Ali Ahmed and Begum Abida Ahmed with President Sadat and Mrs Gihan el Sadat during their visit to Cairo in December 1975.

President Sadat established strong and lasting ties with India during his visit to the country in February 1974. Here he is seen with Prime Minister Indira Gandhi.

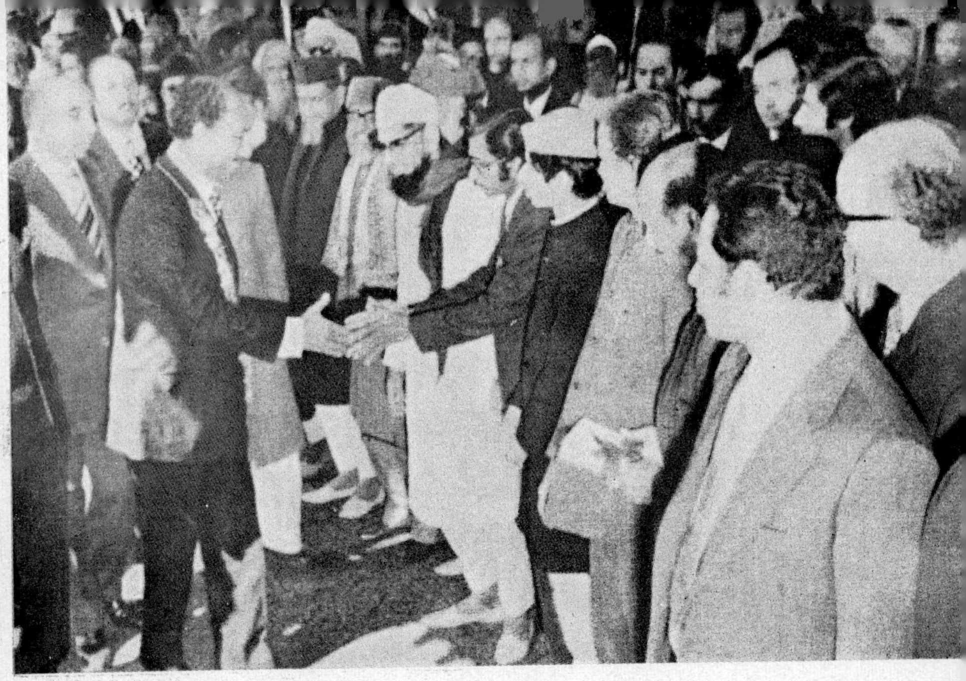

President Sadat meeting members of the Jamiat Ulama-e-Hind on his arrival in Delhi on 24 February 1974. The author (third from right) presented his book *The Fourth Arab-Israeli War* on this occasion.

Paris. Flanked by two guards of honour, the visiting Egyptian President and French President Valery Giscard D'Estaing review French soldiers upon the former's arrival at Orly Airport in January 1975.

Mrs Gihan el Sadat with the Philippines First Lady (second from left) and Dr Aisha Rateb (second from right), the Egyptian Minister for Social Affairs, in Alexandria.

A visit to the Barlev Line in October 1975 by the participants of a seminar in Cairo on the Fourth Arab-Israeli War and its consequences.

An intimate photograph of Sadat with his wife and children. His son, Gamel, is named after Nasser.

Meeting on equal terms. President Sadat is seen in a friendly embrace with Soviet Premier Kosygin.

Mrs Gihan el Sadat has been deeply concerned with the welfare of the armed forces personnel. Below she is feeding a wounded soldier.

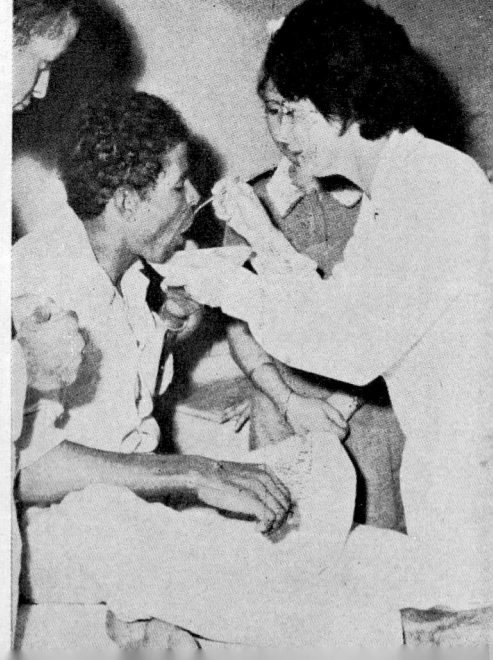

An early photograph of Sadat with Nasser and other leaders of the Revolution.

Half English, half Egyptian, Egypt's First Lady has been a great asset to Sadat. Below is a recent portrait.

President Sadat addresses press correspondents at Palam Airport, New Delhi, before his departure for Dacca, in February 1974.

Sadat with Yasser Arafat. Sadat considers the Palestinian problem as the crux of the Arab-Israeli confrontation. He has stood firm by his commitment to the Palestinian cause.

President Sadat announcing the Sinai agreement providing for Israeli withdrawal from the Sinai passes and the Abu Rudeis oilfields.

Kissinger and Sadat in Alexandria on 1 September 1975 explaining the nature of the Sinai agreement.

President Sadat with President Ford.

A reception accorded to President Nasser, Sadat (then Speaker of the National Assembly), and Zakaria Mohieddin by the Indian Association for Afro-Asian Affairs.

Assad, Sadat, and Arafat in a convivial mood.

The youth of the country joined this dynamic new organisation.[1]

The honeymoon between the Revolutionary Committee and the Muslim Brotherhood was shortlived. When it came to concrete action, Sadat discovered that what the Brotherhood wanted was the merger of the Revolutionary Committee into the Brotherhood and acceptance of everything else which such a course implied. The Revolution had vaster horizons and a broadbased national plan of action and hence the dialogue between Sadat and the Brotherhood came to an abrupt end.

Similarly, Sadat's enthusiasm about the Rashid Ali coup in Iraq setting a pattern for Egypt-German collaboration against the British came to nothing. General Masry had pricked the bubble of such fantasies and meanwhile the young and ebullient Sadat was becoming politically mature. He says:

> The plan of our revolutionary group was as follows: We would carry out a military coup d'etat in Cairo, overthrow the Wafd government under Nahas Pasha and put Ali Maher back in power. The Egyptian army would harry the British forces. We would join up with the Axis troops and the fate of the British empire would be sealed. The Revolutionary Committee assigned to me the task of informing the Muslim Brotherhood our plan. This was some time in July 1942....
>
> I went straight to the point in my conversation with Hassan el Banna. I told him that the time had come for action. I explained our plan and the role which we hoped the followers would play in it....
>
> He had simply promised to support the government without specifying whether this support would be total or partial, material or moral. Finally, he asked me to propose to the Committee that our revolutionary group join the Muslim Brotherhood....[2]
> This was the last interview I had with Hassan el Banna before my arrest and imprisonment. It showed that we had built too high hopes on the Muslim Brotherhood. The truth was that we could rely on nobody to make the revolution but ourselves.

---

[1] *Revolt on the Nile, op. cit.*
[2] *Ibid.*

That Sadat was a close confidant and trusted lieutenant of Nasser is beyond question. Writing in 1957 in a foreword to Sadat's *Revolt on the Nile*, Nasser said:

> Col. Anwar el Sadat is liked and respected. His military virtues, courage and coolness, loyalty and devotion, force of character and disinterestedness, and finally his love of justice, destined him to play a leading role in the Egyptian revolution of July 23, 1952.
>
> He has displayed these qualities throughout his lively career and he put them to the service of our national cause. He was imprisoned for his patriotic activities in November 1942 by the British, and again in 1947. One may imagine how a man of his combative nature suffered under these restraints. Nevertheless these years of captivity gave him leisure to meditate at length upon the conditions to which the Egyptian people had been brought by two thousand years of slavery. He escaped to prove a living symbol of the immense desire for liberation which inspired the peoples of the valley of the Nile.
>
> He fought ceaselessly for his ideals. They were now seeking social justice and the Free Officers, among them Col. Sadat, made every effort to inspire and maintain that faith which was to enable the people to assail their triple enemy: imperialism, monarchy and feudalism.[3]

The 23 July 1952 revolution aimed at securing for Egyptian society justice, stability, peace and freedom, and eliminating imperialism and its allies. Sadat has repeatedly reaffirmed his total dedication to the realization of the original aims of the Egyptian revolution, some of which have been realized and some of which have not. In this respect he has significantly emphasised that the essence of democracy was freedom of the rule of law and the recognition of the right of every individual to express himself individually or collectively within the framework of the law governing society.

Sadat belongs to a family of farmers, a son of the soil, a product of the shovel and the spade, of effort and sweat, deeply attached

---

[3] See Foreword to *Revolt on the Nile*, ibid.

to the waters of the Nile and the traditions of the country. He is a product of the White Revolution which overwhelmed a corrupt monarchy and a despicable imperialism and established social justice, freedom and equality of the people in their rights and responsibilities. As a soldier, Sadat was an outstanding figure among the Free Officers, who tasted the rigours of life and struggle and who could face every challenge with cool calculation and a firm determination, impressing both friends and foes, never compromising on principles or giving them up. If Sadat was a link with the past in the shaping of history, he has been instrumental in triggering a new chain of events with immense potentialities for the future.

The final breach with the Brotherhood came when on 26 October 1954 a prominent member of the Muslim Brotherhood fired eight shots at Nasser who was addressing a large audience in Alexandria. Nasser in perfect equanimity shouted over the microphone, "If one Nasser dies, everyone of you becomes a Nasser." The Revolution had come to stay. In a moment of frustration the Brotherhood had overreached itself and dealt itself a mortal blow.

On 27 July 1954, an agreement was signed between Egypt and Britain for a gradual withdrawal of British troops within a period of twenty months. Nasser made a few concessions like the right of the British to recover the Suez base if any of the Arab powers or Turkey was attacked. This was a matter of tactics. In June 1956 Nasser was elected the President of the Republic with 99 per cent votes.

Desmond Stewart quotes Sadat as having said as follows in his book *Young Egypt:* "Our revolution had been too easy. It was good but it was too easy. I only felt that it became real at the time of Port Said. The fighting sealed it in blood, when we refused to give in, weak though we might be against three powers." The reference was to the tripartite aggression against Egypt in 1956. Port Said was bombarded by British planes. The British had hoped through this action to send a wave of resentment not against themselves but against Nasser and the Free Officers' revolution. They had dubbed Nasser the Hitler of the Nile and had miscalculated that through these tactics they would induce the people of Port Said to disown their own leadership and stage a revolt against the revolution. This proved a farcical expectation. Nasser and Sadat survived. Dulles and Eden had to go.

6

In Defence of the Revolution

The second phase of Sadat's life is that which spans the years between the glorious revolution of 23 July 1952 and Nasser's death on 28 September 1970. Sadat says of this phase in his memoirs:

> After the revolution of 1952 was staged, my responsibility was confined to giving my viewpoint on various matters and implementing the decisions as issued by the Revolutionary Command Council till the year 1956 when Gamal Abdel Nasser was elected president. Still the decisions which I took were on my own responsibility. There is a difference between giving your opinion and making a decision yourself. In the first case the effect is on yourself but in the case of the latter it reflects on the whole nation.

Those were the days when British power was on the decline. They had lost India. Egypt had asserted her own right over the Suez Canal. The war debt had broken the back of the British lion. Britain had already started thinking of withdrawing from the east of Suez, Other powers were entering the game. The warm waters of the Red Sea and the Gulf attracted the Soviet Union. The Mediterranean was fast becoming a White House lake. The USA was irretrievably attracted to the Arab oil basin. Israel became a staging camp for Western entry into the Middle East. A new set of power equations was taking shape. While Nasser was the architect of post revolution policies, Sadat was his trusted lieutenant. In his taped memoirs Sadat has referred to this intimate relationship as being based on his sense of gratitude to Nasser. Nasser, according to Sadat, was a man without personal ambition. Having toiled and struggled for the success of the revolution for over a decade, Nasser had passed the glory to General Neguib who until the last day did not know anything about the revolution. Nasser's selflessness created for him a pan-Arab lobby and Nasserite groups sprang up in a number of Arab countries.

In the early fifties Nasser had for the first time encountered the U. S. Secretary of State over matters of international policy. Egypt under Nasser had not yet cast her lot with either power bloc. The Dullesian anti-communist phobia had expressed itself in the form of the notorious Baghdad Pact. Nasser, however, was unwilling to join this pact which was expected to be a tier of defence against communism in the Middle East. Nasser was violently against any military pacts, U.S.-sponsored or otherwise. In Nasser's view the choice before the Egyptians was not so much between communist and West-sponsored defence pacts as between nationalism and communism. Dulles also considered Nasser a bulwark against communism even though the latter could not openly align himself with any of the West-sponsored anti-communist alliances.

Nasser did not fear any danger from the Soviet Union. His immediate problem was to get rid of the 70,000 British troops who were still in the Canal Zone. The Egyptian army did not have any weapons worth the name for carrying out national defence. Naser's attempt to obtain weapons for national defence had not met with any positive response from the USA and there was considerable dilly-dallying on its part. One of the reasons for this dilly-dallying, as Heikal would have us believe through the pages of *The Cairo Documents*, was Churchill's recommendation to Eisenhower that no arms should be supplied to Egypt as this would be used against the British troops of the Canal Zone. Egypt at the time was reluctant to go in for Soviet weapons, being unused to them. For these reasons Egypt had preferred to obtain the required weapons from the USA Through a series of miscalculations and diplomatic faux pas, the USA missed several opportunities of establishing its credentials with Egypt by acting in time and providing the required weapons. The baseless affronts hurled by

Dulles at the dignity and independence of Egypt led Egypt inevitably to obtain the weapons from the Soviet Union. When the USA realized it, it was too late. The die had been cast. Nasser had joined the non-aligned camp, had attended the Bandung Conference in 1955, had established rapport with the Chinese leaders and had started a dialogue with the Soviet Union.

The Zionists played their due role in sabotaging U.S.-Egyptian relations. Israel was apprehensive lest any U.S. weapons reach Egypt. It was vitally concerned that the relationship between the U.S. and Egypt should remain under a cloud of suspicion and deteriorate with time. Israel did not want any successful Egyptian action against the British garrison in the Suez Canal zone either. The presence of British troops provided a buffer between Egypt and Israel. Secondly, if the British withdrawal from the Canal Zone were brought about, Egyptian attention against Israel would be brought to bear in full. Egypt tried its best to obtain weapons from other sources but what she could obtain was some obsolete or obsolescent weapons of World War II vintage. Obtaining arms supplies without belonging to an alliance of one type or the other was difficult. To add to these difficulties, the arms list prepared by Nasser for national defence was by mistake substituted by the arms list prepared by King Farouk for fighting local insurgency, either by accident or design. The result was a confirmtion of U.S. suspicions about Egypt's intentions.

It is worth noting that Israel also started obtaining her arms supplies from France in 1954. Nasser did not particularly disfavour the supply of French arms to Israel because France could not then bring to bear her full weight of weapons against the Algerian freedom fighters at that time. Egypt had consistently acted in furtherance of the general Arab cause and not within a narrow national frame. Nasser, in an agreement concluded in September 1955 through Prague, laid the basis for Egypt obtaining Soviet weapons. The USA was angry and retaliated by suspending aid to Egypt, cancelling trade agreements with her and severing diplomatic relations. She also promoted a sea blockade of Egypt by preventing ships coming to Egyptian ports with weapon loads.

In mid 1954 Israel did everything possible to spoil Egypt's relations with USA and the UK It also sent a spy to Egypt to sabotage Anglo-U.S. installations in Egypt to promote bad blood between Egypt and the Western democracies. The spy was caught and the sordid affair came to be known as the Lavon Affair. In 1954 Israel started a build-up with French weapons forcing Nasser to go in for Soviet weapons. The U.S. reaction was retaliatory and as usual clumsy. They backed out of their commitment to help Egypt in constructing the Aswan Dam. The Soviet Union took this opportunity to plug the gap and promised to come to the aid of Egypt where the USA had failed.

Nasser recognised Communist China in the year 1956. This further infuriated the West and Churchill is said to have remarked that if Nasser was posing a threat to the Middle East oil then it was time he should go. Nasser in turn pointed out that as the oil producing states took 50 per cent of the oil profits, Egypt would be justified in taking 50 per cent of the Canal transit profits. A crisis was brewing between the arrogant West and a self-respecting Nasser who would accept neither their dictation nor tutelage. Now he would not stop at 50 per cent of the Canal earnings. Why should Egypt be denied her full share of Canal earnings? Nasser had made up his mind and his innermost circle was taken into confidence. The Suez Canal was nationalised on 26 July 1956. This provoked a violent Anglo-French reaction which was anticipated by Nasser. A conference known as the London Conference was convened on 16 August 1956 at which India's representative, Krishna Menon, presented Egypt's case with great eloquence. The stage was now set for tripartite aggression against Egypt. On 31 October 1956 Cairo was bombed heralding the joint Zionist-imperialist action. The glorious Egyptian resistance which followed thereafter against overwhelming odds is now a part of history.

1960 and 1961 saw a cooling off of Egyptian-Soviet relations for various reasons, the chief being Nasser's action against local communists. Nasser met Krushchev to sort out their misunderstandings. Sadat was then the Speaker of the National Assembly. In May 1962 Sadat led an Egyptian parliamentary delegation to Moscow to participate in the May Day celebrations. At a reception at the Kremlin, Sadat made a formal speech thanking the Soviet Union and expressing his hope that this friendship would grow. Krushchev in his speech, however, overreached himself and passionately declared that Arab nationalism was not the final answer and only communism could deliver the goods. He added that jails could not chain the doctrine of communism. This was an oblique criticism of the way Egypt was tackling her problems on the basis of Arab nationalism and not communism.

When Sadat returned home he reported the matter to Nasser and they decided that Krushchev's remarks should be answered. Sadat wrote a letter to Krushchev in whch he repudiated the latter's arguments by saying that he had himself spent six years in prison fighting for freedom without changing his opinions. Nasser's Egypt of 1964 was symbolic of the Arab-African resurgence, and Nasser was riding the crest of popularity. The success of his experiment and the popularity of his policies once again attracted Krushchev who became affable and curious about the appeal of Arab nationalism as evidenced in Egypt.

Sadat figured again when Marshal Abdullah el Sallal, Chief of the Palace Guard, overthrew the Imam el Badr of Yemen. Sallal had been imprisoned by the Imam for five years. During his imprisonment Sallal was treated like a dog chained to a peg and food was thrown at him. Sallal's sympathisers came to Egypt and met Sadat, then the Speaker of the National Assembly. It was at Sadat's recommendation that support was given to Sallal and Egypt assumed the responsibility for supporting Yemen in all respects. The experiment, thought to be temporary, snowballed into an expensive and long drawn out campaign, and Nasser had to send a Division to cover a battalion.

In 1955 Sadat became a Minister of State. He was also the Secretary General of the Islamic Conference and the editor of *El Gomhouria*, a daily. Talking of those days Sadat was nostalgic and recounted this interesting anecdote about India in his address to the National Assembly on 14 March 1976.

I am reminded of a story, derived from our society, and which illustrates what I am trying to say. Twenty-one years ago, in 1955, I was a Minister of State. I was also Secretary-General of the Islamic Conference, and as such, I travelled to many Islamic countries in Asia and upto Indonesia.

On my way back, I visited India where Pandit Nehru was then Prime Minister and leader of India following independence. Pandit Nehru gave a reception in my honour, and as we stood receiving and greeting the guests, a man and his wife arrived. They were both members of the Indian People's Assembly. They have two houses in the People's Assembly in India, House of

Commons and a Senate. The couple I am speaking of were members of the House of Commons and I had already met them when they had passed through Cairo. They were members of the Communist Party, and they had started a violent attack against Nehru in Parliament. When they came in, he introduced them as Mr and Mrs so and so, and I said that they were old friends of mine. They both embraced Nehru while he turned to me saying 'Beware of these two...don't let them turn you Bolshevik and a Communist...they have caused me a great deal of trouble and are members of the Opposition.' Indeed they were causing Nehru worry and trouble, but before me, the strangers, the man and his wife, kissed Nehru on both cheeks in his capacity as Father of India and head of the family, regardless of opposition to him in political work.

When I returned to Cairo in 1955, I found the struggle had reached its peak, in the Revolution Command Council—Which remained until 1965, I handed in my resignation and wrote in it this story.

I said that in India that had more than 10 languages, 20 religions and 20 races and nationalities, with a population of 400 million at the time, despite the differences in religion, faith, race, and origin, they all agreed on the point that Nehru was the Father of India and the head of the family. Because of that, India with its population of 400 million, was a cohesive state, as it adopted the family system.

I handed in my resignation in 1955 and the members of the Revolution Command Council discussed the matter with me. I suggested that we follow the same system (as India) as the struggle pointed to the fact that being young men, of nearly the same age and nearly the same position, since we were all members of the Revolution Command Council, there was bound to be struggle between us. I was against struggle and was of the opinion that we should have a head of the family. Apart from that, we were all free to express our opinions, as in India they did with Nehru.

In 1956 Arab public opinion was fully with Nasser. Arab solidarity had undoubtedly been achieved. Egypt was selected by Israel for attack as she was the most important Arab country in the vanguard of the Arab struggle. Israeli aggression was launched against Egypt not because the latter had concluded a defence pact with Jordan and Syria but because she had started importing Soviet weapons in a big way and was fast becoming an acknowledged pan-Arab leader. Nationalisation of the Suez Canal was only an excuse for aggression.

The aggressors knew that Egypt at that time did not have the resources to face the tripartite powers militarily. This aggressive act, however, secured for Egypt great political gains which compensated for her military losses. The unity which emerged between Egypt and Syria in 1958 was a logical result of the crystallisation of Arab nationalism of Nasser's dream.

The dissolution of Syrian-Egyptian unity came as a great and sad shock to Nasser. Nasser wanted to foster and cement progressive Arab nationalism through his war in Yemen for which Egypt made great sacrifices in men and material. Within twenty-four hours of the outbreak of hostilities between Israel and Egypt in 1967, the Egyptian army had to be pulled back from Yemen. Egypt was thus forced to suffer big losses both in the Yemen and Sinai operations which had to be compensated by a new phase of rearmament. This price was paid by Egypt because she assumed the role of leader for a progressive pan-Arab struggle. If as a result of this, Egypt was saddled with enormous economic burdens it should not surprise anyone.

Nasser in *The Philosophy of the Revolution* spoke of the various concentric circles around Egypt, the foremost being the Arab circle. Secondly, the circle of the continent of Africa from whose heart the Nile flowed, and thirdly, the Islamic circle, a religion, a civilisation and a heritage which bound Egyptian Muslims to Muslims all over the world. The Muslim population stood at roughly one-sixth of the total world population and extended from the Atlantic Ocean to the Pacific. With its all-embracing monotheism and a comprehensive legal system any developments in any part of the Islamic world had repercussions on other parts.

7

Sadat Blazes a New Trail

28 September 1970 was a day of disaster for the Arab world. Nasser passed away all of a sudden. The scene is best described by Sadat himself in his *Memoirs*.

> I was fully informed of Nasser's illness and its complications which he had managed to keep secret since the defeat in the June 1967 War. Still I never expected that he would die so soon. His death came as a violent surprise to me which I had not taken into calculation. We had got used to Nasser as a part of life which would not change. I even firmly believed that Nasser would survive me and his other colleagues. His personality appeared so robust that we took it to be stronger than death and I never calculated the immense vacuum which the passing away of Nasser would create or that one day I would find myself compelled to bear responsibility to fill this vacuum.
>
> Nasser's death occurred on Monday, the 28 September 1970, the day on which the Arab Summit Conference held in Cairo ended. The Conference had been convened to put an end to the confrontation between the Palestinian commandos and the Jordanian government. According to the usual convention, Nasser, as the Head of the host country, saw the Kings and Heads of States off at the Cairo International Airport. The late King Feisal and the Emir of Kuwait were the last to leave. Nasser showed much evidence of exhaustion while seeing King Feisal off. This

was attributed to the extreme tension which prevailed during the conference and to the extraordinary effort he had exerted to put an end to bloodshed in Jordan.

I knew that Alexandria was the only place which would give Nasser physical and mental solace. So I asked his private secretary, Mohammed Ahmed, to make arrangements for our travel to Alexandria the following day. To spare Nasser more exertion, I suggested that I should deputise for him in seeing the Emir of Kuwait off. The Emir was a personal friend of mine and I was sure he would not mind. But Nasser decided to bid farewell to the Kuwaiti guest himself and then take rest. Nasser was evidently haggard. He escorted the Kuwaiti Emir to the plane to where we could wave to the departing guest. But Nasser was unable to move away after the Emir had ascended the plane. He sweated profusely and his face turned extremely yellow. He asked for his car to come over to him where he stood and he took it without waiting to wave to the guest.

I still thought the trouble was nothing more than exhaustion and I told him before he left that we would go to Alexandria the following day. Nasser agreed. I went back home for rest but at around 7 p.m. I was awakened by a telephone call from Nasser's home. Nasser was somewhat exhausted, the message said, and I was required to see him. On arriving at Nasser's Manchiet El Bakri residence I learnt the stunning news that Nasser had passed away an hour before, despite the frantic efforts by a team of doctors who tried their best to avert the catastrophe.

Self-control was expedient in such a situation especially when the fate of a people was at stake. I ordered the body to be immediately moved to Qubba Palace where it was decided to hold an emergency Cabinet meeting with the Higher Executive Committee. Burial arrangements were agreed upon. The funeral was fixed for three days later to enable the Kings and Heads of States to attend it. The text of an announcement on Nasser's death to the outside world was also agreed upon...

Even at that meeting manoeuvres by some interested parties had started. The provisional constitution enforced at that time had provided that the first Vice-President would succeed the President. I had been appointed the sole deputy of the President and there was no second deputy. The post of first Vice President had been provided for in the 1964 constitution because of Nasser's desire that Abdul Hakim Amer should be his first deputy in the event of other deputies being appointed. Actually other deputies had been appointed but did not hold their posts for long and later on only one Vice President remained.

When I was appointed Vice President in December 1969, I was the only Deputy President but some people at that meeting tried to refer to the rigid provision in the Constitution that the President's successor shall be the First Deputy and not the only Deputy. The objection was so absurd that it received absolutely no support at the meeting but still it had its special significance, for it underlined the cross-currents and conflicts which were about to surface soon.

As a matter of fact I did not think at that time of holding presidential elections. Nasser in his speech on 10 June, 1967, had declared that he would resume Presidency at the people's behest and that presidential elections would be held immediately after the consequences of Israeli aggression were liquidated. I thought on the same lines. I wanted to continue as a Vice-President or Acting President until the aggressed territory was vacated whereupon the people could elect their President through free and democratic elections.

However, on the evening of Wednesday, 30 September 1970, I changed my mind after sensing the various manoeuvres which were going on....

Nasser had a feeling of his untimely death. This explains why he summoned me to his home on the day of his departure to Morocco in December 1969 to attend the Arab Summit there. He told me of his fears of confusion in the country should anything happen to him and made me take the oath as Vice President. The news was officially announced at that time. This action of Nasser indicated his desire that the nation should maintain its continuity in its forward march.

Nasser did not heed the campaign of rumours launched by the centres of power against me after my appointment. They wanted to damage my image and prevent Nasser from handing over responsibility to me gradually. Nasser's intention was clear when he invited me to attend a military meeting at the General Headquarters where our defence plan, known as Plan 200, was discussed. Apart from Nasser and myself, the Soviet experts also attended it. For seven hours we heard commanders report on their roles in the plan and the meeting ended with the finding that the plan was hundred per cent sound. Abdel Nasser wanted me to be fully informed of all affairs including sharing with him the responsibility for Egypt's defence plan.

A piece of advice from a friend and a colleague is worth mentioning here. Brother Houari Boumedienne, the Algerian President, had arrived in Cairo before the funeral and we had a two-hour meeting. He tendered me advice which I still remember. I had told him of my desire not to hold presidential elections, preferring to act as Deputy or Acting President just as Nasser had planned. Boumedienne strongly objected saying that there must be absolutely no doubt about stability in Egypt because of its high standing in the Arab world and the heavy responsibilities she bore on account of her circumstances. He advised that presidential elections should be held immediately.

Boumedienne's advice looked plausible in view of the manoeuvres and undercurrents which as I said had begun to surface only two days after Nasser passed away. Some power centres in the Higher Executive Committee had started conspiring and claimed that they were the legal heirs to Abdel Nasser.

On the date of the funeral I was so exhausted that I could not accompany the funeral procession. I collapsed and was administered five injections which left me unconscious for hours. When I recovered, Abdel Nasser had already been buried, and one of the most momentous pages of the Egyptian contemporary history had been turned. I began thinking thoroughly of the onerous historical responsibility which had so suddenly and unexpectedly descended on me.

The same day, i.e., Thursday, I moved from the Qubba Palace to that little house called Oruba Palace in Heliopolis to be close to the scene of events. In the afternoon, I called in the senior responsible officials, Shaarawi Gomaa and Sami Sharaf. I told them that I had changed my mind about remaining Vice-President or Acting President and that I had ddecided to hold early elections for Presidency.

In addition to undercurrents of conflict and subtle manoeuvres and brother Boumedienne's advice, a new element came to the fore which decided the issue once for all.

This was a message from the Armed Forces which said emphatically that they must have a responsible Supreme Commander in the critical circumstances through which the country was passing when parts of the country's territory were still under occupation.

I called in Shaarawi Gomaa on Thursday afternoon and ordered him in his capacity as Interior Minister and Secretary for Organisation in the Arab Socialist Union, to prepare for a meeting of the ASU Higher Executive Committee on Saturday to name a President for the ASU Central Committee at its meeting two days later. I had to take cognisance of nomination before its submission to the People's Assembly thus completing the nomination formalities. The Presidential elections, I said, would be held on the Thursday following the People's Assembly meeting. By thus arranging for elections exactly two weeks after Nasser's burial, the vacuum could be filled which otherwise would have weakened the country at a critical time.

The power centres were displeased with my decision to go ahead with the nomination for Presidency. They did not show any open resentment however, as they expected an opportunity which would enable them to turn the tables against me.

On the day following Nasser's burial, which was a Friday, opposition manoeuvres began taking a tangible shape. Two from this powerful group came to the Oruba Palace to meet me. They expressed fears that in the meeting of the Higher Executive Committee fixed for Saturday there could be a possible rift. Some had objections to the holding of Presidential elections barely two weeks after Nasser's burial. They said that there was no need for such indecent haste in holding elections only two weeks after Nasser's burial as it would appear that there was the intention for getting one particular person elected.

I was, however, emphatic and told the two delegates that in my capacity as deputy to the President I had already decided to hold the elections. The late President had entrusted the Republic to me and I could not betray this trust whatever may be the manoeuvres of interested power groups. I pointed out that the people alone were the arbiters in electing a President whoever he may be. In the meantime I told them that I would firmly deal with opposition tactics and manoeuvres which defied our Constitution and our traditions with a heavy hand.

My intellectual relations with Nasser had a direct bearing on the years of decision. According to convention laid down by

Nasser, a Prime Minister had to be nominated to the Arab Socialist Union Central Committee. Acting according to this convention I nominated Dr Mahmoud Fawzi as Prime Minister at the Central Committee's first meeting following Nasser's death. The meeting was held on 5 October 1970. The nomination did not meet with the favour either of the power centres or by some members of the ASU Higher Committee who coveted premiership. I wanted to make things quite clear and told them in all frankness that I could not follow the same procedures as Nasser had followed before me but this I pointed out did not mean that I differed with Nasser on basic principles. It meant only that we differed on ways and means to achieve the same objectives. I told them that the people expected me to achieve our national objectives as cherished by Nasser. The people at the same time did not wish that I should be a carbon copy of Nasser, for human nature does not permit such duplication.

I recalled that I had long meetings with Nasser at his home or mine, which continued almost until his death. Nasser appreciated and accepted my differences with him on the means to be adopted but I deemed it wise not to publicise such differences for I hated manoeuvres and display of muscles. I also pointed out that the country required a man who would be fully responsible for his decisions and be accountable before the people.

In my differences with Nasser over the means and methods I was not negative. All through the year 1970, until he passed away, I argued with him on the need for changing the line of action which had led us to the defeat of 1967. Our great people held fast after the setback of 1967 and reinstated Gamal Abdel Nasser as a symbol of national solidarity. The people therefore had the right to choose a policy which suited the fundamental values which they cherished and which differed from the line of action which led us to the debacle of 1967.

The people deemed it necessary to introduce a change in policy even on 10 June 1967, the day when the people returned Gamal Abdel Nasser to power and took some steps in that direction.

Nasser's way of government produced developments which were dictated by Nasser's own nature. These developments had affected the Revolutionary Command Council since the first years of the revolution and I was surprised to receive a suggestion after Nasser's death by a number of friends from among the old Revolutionary Command Council advising that I should turn the clock back and return to the point where we started 20 years ago instead of continuing on our journey. Such an action was unthinkable.

The suggestion proposed the return of the old Revolutionary Command Council to rule the country for one year through the institution of a constituent assembly and that I in my capacity as Vice President should head the Revolutionary Command Council pending presidential elections. The Constituent Assembly would in the meantime prepare a Constitution.

This meant that the country should remain as it was at the time of Nasser's death and that we should enter an era of domestic conflicts while the enemy knocked at Egypt's doors. Election of a President from among the members of the old Revolutionary Command Council would have meant only strife because of personal affiliations. Naturally I turned down the suggestion to avert such conflicts within the Council which had brewed even as far back as 1954.

The Presidential elections were duly held and I received the result on 16 October 1970. Immediately upon my election I began consultations on the formation of a cabinet and on the form of government. I made it clear from the very beginning that I could not and would not agree to the concentration of power in one hand now that an opportunity had offered itself for the redistribution of authority and responsibility through the institutions of a Prime Minister and a ASU Secretary.

Almost 20 years of my experience with government taught me that things could not be managed properly through one person. This happened in the case of Gamal Abdel Nasser. He was human and could not possibly get acquainted with all matters all by himself.

The emergence of centres of power was the outcome of Nasser's concentration of power in his hands. This gave some of his aides an opportunity to exclusively manage the affairs of the sector under their direct charge with the result that gross mistakes were committed and wrongly attributed to Nasser.

I was determined to form a homogeneous team which would assume responsibility with a sense of patriotism, cooperation and sacrifice in the best interests of Egypt above any other consideration. I thanked Almighty God for having enabled me to accomplish this task after five years of hardship in 1975.

I must state that I am indebted to Nasser and fully grateful to him now that we are in the process of an objective appraisal of Nasser's great struggle. We differed only on the means but agreed on basic values and objectives.

Sadat was comparatively unknown internationally at the time of Nasser's death. The prevailing mood among the members of the inner circle of Nasser was to settle down for some sort of a collective exercise of authority since no single individual was thought suitable to take his place. Among the members of his inner circle were Ali Sabri, reputed to be a leftist, General Mohammed Fawzi, the Defence Minister, not known to have any political ambitions, Sharawi Gomaa, the Interior Minister who lacked a political base and Mohammed Fayek, the Minister of Information, and others who belonged to the higher echelons of the police service. In that conglomeration none was considered outstanding enough to step into Nasser's shoes. The least controversial among them at that time and by far the most acceptable was Sadat. The other two prominent figures such as Zakaria Mohieuddin, the person whom Nasser had nominated for presidency when he had resigned on 10 June 1967 following the debacle, was not popular with the inner circle, and Hussain el Shafei was vice-president who did not hold any political position during Nasser's time.

On 13 May 1971, the members of the inner circle appear to have decided to eject Sadat from the presidency but without much thought or planning. They announced their collective resignation over the radio and there was confusion in the administrative apparatus. It was not clear who was in power and whose orders were being broadcast. Sadat took charge and ordered the group's arrest. Sadat's assumption of full control cleared the fog. In subsequent investigations and trials it emerged that the opposition had planned to attribute certain political failures to Sadat and challenge his continuity in office. They opposed, for example, the unity of Libya and Egypt, then being negotiated, without Syria joining it. They advocated another war with Israel with active Soviet participation. Sadat was said to be an obstruction in these matters.

The few months between September 1970 and May 1971, were not adequate to assess the political achievements of Sadat or to judge his policies and programmes. They seemed more like excuses than reasons at that time. The principal reason was that the various centres of power wanted to retain their hold. The fact that Sadat eased them out and there was hardly any public reaction to their ouster, showed that both singly and jointly they lacked either a mass base or failed to carry conviction with the masses. The means they had adopted for achieving their ends were also ill-conceived. It did not appear to be a well planned coup which could ensure credibility and continuity of the political struggle in Egypt. It appeared to be a slipshod affair engineered at the spur of the moment. Nevertheless, it involved persons who were in positions of authority, both in the Arab Socialist Union and in the administrative and police services. Sadat needed an effective base and a political platform. He availed of the opportunity to reorganise both the political structure as well as the security services.

This period was crucial for Soviet-Egyptian relations, for a leftist inspired coup was taking place in the Sudan at about the same time and the official Egyptian sympathies were with the Sudanese president, Jafar Numeri. This must have caused misgivings in the Soviet capital. Podgorny visited Egypt at the time and signed a fifteen year treaty of friendship and cooperation. The negotiations which were taking place between Libya and Egypt on the one hand and the Egyptian support for President Numeri against a leftist coup attempt were not happy developments for Soviet-Egyptian relations. Sadat's position appeared weak at home and the deterioration of relations with the Soviet Union seemed unfortunate. The Soviet policy sought naturally to strengthen its relationship with other allies in the area, viz. Syria, a Mediterranean-based country and Iraq, a Gulf-based country to make up for it. This tended to improve the Soviet position both in the Mediterranean and the Gulf and tended to combat the Chinese who were seeking a hold in the Gulf area.

Sadat's relationship with Qaddafi began on a hopeful note, but soon ended up ignominiously. Egypt badly needed Libyan funds and the latter's federation with Egypt would have given Libya the much-needed political boost to her position. Qaddafi thought of himself as a leader without a country. Libyan territory without the contiguous parts of Egypt and the Sudan was strategically not vital. Nasser had considered Libyan territory as providing depth to Egypt. The negotiations which went on between Sadat and Qaddafi enhanced Qaddafi's political importance. Nevertheless, the negotiations either for a merger or the formation of a federation did not make any headway because of the Libyan unwillingness to get down to specific commitments. They seemed to carry on protracted negotiations endlessly. Moreover, Qaddafi's various statements and postures smacked of imbalance. Despite his basic sincerity he was mercurial and unpredictable. Sadat's relationship with him had given rise to suspicions in the traditionalist Arab countries of the Gulf and Saudi Arabia which looked askance at Libyan-Egyptian attempts at unity. The insurgency movements aided and abetted by Qaddafi in the Gulf area was not to their liking. Sadat ultimately decided to diassociate himself from the flirtation with Libya. He realized that it was far more important to stand on firm ground and coordinate political and financial policies with traditionalist countries like Saudi Arabia and the Gulf countries than expose his political and economic fortunes to the unsteady and fluctuating postures of Libya.

Sadat's cooperation with King Fiesal indicated his realism and political maturity. Saudi Arabia enjoyed a unique political and spiritual importance in the Muslim world and its ruler enjoyed a special status among the Muslims. The enormous oil power of Saudi Arabia was of vital concern to the West and the United States. The U.S.A. and Saudi Arabia therefore needed each other. Ideologically the traditionalist Saudi Arabia could not be close to the Soviet Union. The various liberation struggles around Saudi Arabia could not have been a welcome development in King Feisal's calculations. The Saudi army could not feel self-esteem while Israel not only occupied big chunks of Arab territory but also Jerusalem. The holy shrines were King Feisal's special responsibility. Part of the Saudi forces were with Jordan and in the context of the storm of political unrest raging in the Gulf the monarchies had to adopt a more radical posture and show positive gains both to ensure their own survival as well as make a positive contribution to the Arab struggle as a whole.

Nasser's campaign in Yemen had soured Egyptian-Saudi relations in the past. The disaster of the 1967 War, however, had brought about a fundamental change in the situation necessitating the suspension of Egyptian operations in Yemen. Sadat realized that it was important to marshal the immense potential of Saudi Arabia to achieve Arab ends. The Saudi Arabian monetary resources, her oil reserves, her influence with the USA, and her burning desire to employ its armed forces against the usurper of the Islamic holy shrine of Jerusalem, were all positive factors which had not hitherto been harnessed for the furtherance of the common Arab cause. The Saudi Arabian army needed an honourable and worthwhile role to play in the promotion of the general Arab cause.

Let alone an abrupt stoppage of oil, even the threat of stabilising or even reducing the quantity of oil extracted by Saudi Arabia was an effective enough threat to discourage the West from continuing in their discredited oil policy of blindly supporting Israel against even genuine Arab demands. Collaboration between Sadat and King Feisal appears to have been intimate and is a standing monument of Sadat's new style in breaking out of the groove and establishing a formidable Arab grouping which could instead influence Western policies decisively. Egypt could not hope to get any financial assistance unless she had plans to recover her lost territory by force. Sadat was clear that going to war was the only honourable answer. He had made up his mind.

The 1967 War had proved disastrous for King Hussain who not only had lost the West Bank and Jerusalem but also an effective part of his tank force. Thousands of refugees had flooded Jordan and the Palestinians had made Jordan their base for operations against the West Bank. Both Iraqi and Syrian troops were inside Jordanian territory and several serious clashes had taken place between the Jordanian and Palestinian forces resulting in the famous massacre of Black September when over a thousand Palestinians were killed and many more captured. This had isolated Jordan from the rest of the Arab world.

Sadat's concern about Jordan emanated from its strategic borders with Israel which were vital for any operations against Israel. In his view it was even more important to stop the shedding of Arab blood by a brother Arab. It was not, however, easy because what had already happened had done irreparable damage to the Arab cause. When the Jordanian Premier Wasifi el Tel was murdered in Cairo by the Palestinians, Sadat abstained from acting against the assassins. Sadat opposed Hussein's plan of accepting Moshe Dayan's theory of open bridges and entering into a settlement with the Israeli authorities about the West Bank. Hussein's plan announced in March 1973 was rejected by Sadat and Jordanian-Egyptian relations were severed. It was not until later 1973 that

Sadat felt obliged to bring Jordan back into the Arab fold and make King Hussein take his place in the coming period of confrontation. Sadat played a positive role in bringing about a reconciliation between King Hussein and the Gulf countries just before the Ramadan War. Past experience could not but have imposed understandable caution on King Hussein's part even during the Ramadan War. He appeared reluctant to make commitments beyond positioning part of his forces along his long frontiers with Israel and some troops south of Jerusalem. This could at least tie down a part of the Israeli forces on these fronts. Sadat's mind was wholly absorbed in the coming war and the role he had visualised for each Arab country.

1971 and 1972 were crucial years in the life of Sadat and that of Egypt. It was a period of uncertainty and doubt which continued until October 1973. This was a period when the 20,000 Russian experts seeping down to Brigade level had overstayed their welcome despite their valuable contribution in preparing Egypt for defence. During the war of attrition Egypt had been subjected to a series of escalations. The Egyptian bombardment of Israeli positions had led to two results. Deep Israeli air raids necessitated the erection of an effective network of anti-aircraft defence through missiles. The Canal Zone itself became a fortified position. There is no doubt that the Soviet air-defence missile system gave some teeth to the Egyptian air defence network which the Israeli aircraft could not easily penetrate even though the lack of offensive weapons such as ground-to-ground missiles and advanced sophisticated Migs such as Mig 23 did not give Egypt a capacity to conduct offensive operations deep within Israel. The Russians, firstly, did not want an escalation of the conflict in view of detente, and secondly, they were not sure that Egypt would be able to effectively absorb and utilise any more sophisticated equipment.

In 1971 and 1972, which were called years of decision by Sadat, nothing much had happened to justify calling them years of decision. This had created only a credibility gap in leadership and exposed Sadat to both domestic as well as foreign criticism and ridicule. There was student unrest and the armed forces were chary of being overloaded by the Soviet experts. The closure of the Canal ever since 1967 had resulted in the Egyptian economy being deprived of an annual income of $ 500 million. Egypt was made to feel a pensioner of Saudi Arabia, Libya, and Kuwait who were compensating Egypt and Syria for this loss. Even this was subject to the changing political climate as was evident from the suspension of the Libyan contribution to the Fund. The Egyptian economy was in the doldrums. Its burdens as well as the population were increasing.

Israel was firmly entrenched in the saddle. Her strategic appreciation of ensuring security by decisive and swift military action before the super powers intervened had paid rich dividends in the past. She had come to believe in her invincibility in the face of Arab weakness and disunity. The western news media had added to this state of demoralisation by predicting the fall of Sadat any moment. There was nothing which the Arab governments, particularly in the confrontation states, had to show to the people by way of achievement. In this atmosphere of gloom and defidence Sadat took over the reins of Egyptian and Arab leadership. His leadership faced a severe test. When and where was he to start? Sadat, however, was clear in his own mind but what about the general public? He ignored the doubting Thomases and set his sails with clarity and precision. He started building a domestic base to consolidate his power at home. He achieved this by liquidating the centres of power and reorganising the Arab Socialist Union. He despatched the 20,000 Russian experts back home. This achieved two results. The army leadership at home no longer felt cramped in their style of functioning, and the decision showed him to be free of outside influence in formulating his day-to-day policies. More important than all this was the sense of absolute complacency which he induced in Israel. Israel had almost written off Egypt from her military map as being of any consequence. Looking through the other end of the telescope and with the wisdom of hindsight it is possible today to appreciate the forethought displayed by Sadat in this respect, and the enormous lengths to which he went in deliberately fostering a sense of complacency in the Israeli ranks before he launched his great step of the crossing of the Suez Canal. Sadat's action brought about changes on the international scene which had scarcely been anticipated by anyone. Detente came under severe strain. Some commentators went so far as to say that Sadat sabotaged detente as detente did not suit the Egyptian and Arab aims in the Middle East. Sadat says the following in his *Memoirs* about the situation he faced:

I assumed responsibility after the death of Nasser when Egypt was a country torn apart. The regime was divided between conflicting forces; the hold of Israel controlled our fate and foreign forces tried to impose their guardianship and their will upon us. Poverty was rampant. We were almost begging for arms and we were about to beg for bread as well. I prayed to God not to put such burdens on me which were beyond my capacity to bear. I sought Almighty God's help while I was perplexed and sought His guidance on where I could start. The centres of power accentuated the conflict when I took my first major decision of liquidating the centres of power which aimed at breaking the regime and stopping our forward march.

The decision was not an easy one since the difficulty lay in finding a replacement for someone you wanted to remove. It also involved my ability to judge the person and pass the verdict even though I had known the person very well and had worked with him before his removal. The background to this decision was complex and went back to many years before my assuming power and shouldering full responsibility.

To go to war is a serious decision and one can hardly appreciate the burdens and conflicts which a responsible person feels while making such a decision although I have lived the life of an army officer, lived through war, or prepared myself for war. I took many decisions when I was away from the army appearing on national campaigns involving the use of arms but these were minor compared to the responsibility of launching the nation and the armed forces into war.

War was a chance and fortunes fluctuate in war. None could guarantee the outcome of the war yet there was urgency about the Egyptian capability to fight. I was and am fully confident of our armed forces. After conducting a minute analysis of the 1967 War, I was confident that our armed forces were the victims of circumstances and not the cause of the defeat. I met our officers and soldiers after Egypt had recovered from the defeat of 1967. I discovered that Egypt was able to fight not merely on the battlefield but on the entire Egyptian territory. This outstanding conclusion supported my decision to prepare for war. It was a decision which reflected the will of every Egyptian as if it was his individual decision.

Every soldier wanted to fight and this was not because he was merely carrying out a decision imposed on him. This was the spirit behind the miracle of the crossing operations. This part of history needs to be recorded for the benefit of this generation and the generations to come.

I bore the responsibility after a lot of inner struggle to seek the right path. I then took the second main decision to do without the Soviet experts. I was hesitant before taking this decision. Egypt was in need of the Soviet friendship. Could I maintain this friendship and develop it? My hesitation resulted from my national responsibility towards Egypt. I could not be a dutiful son of Egypt when Egyptian territory remained under Israeli occupation and I remained without doing anything about it. However, I took the decision of dispensing with the Soviet experts, the details of which I cannot mention here.

Sadat is reported to have sent a letter to Brezhnev on 22 September 1973 presumably about the coming war. He met the Soviet Ambassador Vinogradov, in Cairo on 4 October 1973. There was thus very little time for the Soviet Union to react to the outbreak of war. The main worry of the Soviet Union was to let the Arab-Israeli confrontation remain a regional affair and not spill over to affect the detente adversely. There is, therefore, something to be said for Sadat's claim that the decision to go to war was purely his and thus "hundred per cent Egyptian." While both the Soviet Union and the USA manoeuvred to play their respective roles of support to the two contestants they also took care to preserve detente all the same. What is important, however, is to note that whatever the assessment of the U.S. and Soviet leaders may have been, none of the Israeli leaders expected a serious war to break out on 6 October 1973.

In order to appreciate the manner in which Sadat kept his secret it is necessary to briefly survey the Israeli theory of her security and where and how it went wrong in the case of the Ramadan War. Israel was all along sensitive to any threat developing on two fronts at the same time. At the slightest sign of unity emerging between the two fronts, Israel believed in making a preemptive strike against the stronger country to put the whole plan out of gear. They would then be free to deal a military blow to the other country. Another basis of the Israeli theory of security was to finish off military operations quickly well before super power intervention became imminent. Her military gains would then be used to bargain for peace for a considerable length of time. Israel would inflict sufficient damage on Arab equipment, and the Arabs would take an enormously long time to recoup.

The developments which had taken place after June 1967 were not entirely to the satisfaction of the Israelis. The Suez Canal zone had become virtually a defensive line of great merit and invincibility. The Israelis had tried their best to prevent these defensive works coming up by their constant aerial bombardment but without the desired effect. The Egyptians persisted and brought to bear their superior heavy artillery strength on the Israeli positions in the Sinai. The Israeli air strikes could not make up for their deficiency in heavy artillery. The result was deeper and deeper Israeli air raids into Egyptian territory to attack the Egyptian artillery positions and the missile networks which were coming up. That the Egyptians were able to build up and establish a missile network and maintain there gun positions showed their perseverance in the face of Israeli attacks. The missile defensive network established by the Egyptians in the face of constant interference by Israeli air close to the Suez Canal, and its conversion into a formidable defensive fortification was to the credit of the Egyptian High Command. The achievement of Sadat lay in the fact that he manoeuvred himself in such a way that the Israeli theory of security could not hold good this time. It is true that any Israeli pre-emptive strike would have disrupted Arab plans but at successive levels within the Israeli High Command the consensus appeared to be not to carry out a pre-emptive strike as in the opinion of Golda Meir it would have alienated Israel from the international comity of nations and the USA would have been hindered in rushing effective assistance to her.

According to Dayan, the Israelis did not want to spend £10 million for mobilisation unless they were sure of Egyptian intentions. This time Sadat certainly did save £10 m for Dayan. Dayan considered skeleton regular forces could be summoned from the rear. Such was the Israeli miscalculation that they even considered militarised settlements on the borders as another line of defence. It remained for Sadat to shatter Israeli's complacency for all time. Sadat not only neutralised the strong points in the enemy's armoury both politically and militarily but also exploited to the full the basic weaknesses in their concepts of security. The static Barlev defence line mentality had playe dhavoc with the Israeli concept. The Israeli armed forces which prided themselves on their blitzkrieg capacity were now distributed into thin penny packets on static defence lines such as the Barlev Line which could not even buy enough time for their reserve units to be mobilised. King Hussein was right when he asserted recently that the technological gap between the Israeli soldier and the Arab soldier was fast filling up.

As regards the argument that the Israeli leaders by and large did not want to carry out a pre-emptive strike is invalidated by Kissinger's remarks that the real reason was the Israelis never expected war to break out. In fact if the Israelis had expected any major Arab moves they would have set into motion counter measures well in advance and not contrived a last minute alibi. Whatever the reasons there is no doubt that Sadat, for the first time, had meticulously planned his moves. After taking into consideration all that human ingenuity could provide in meeting a certain situation, a stroke of luck also helped Sadat. Sadat, who had planned for 26,000 casualties, was happy beyond measure when the actual figure was a minute fraction of it.

A word about Sadat's role in conducting the Ramadan War will not be out of place. After having effected the initial crossing, the Egyptian forces played cautious. Their operations were slow and well within the missile cover provided by the Canal Zone defences. The Syrian front on the other hand was suffering heavy casualties and the Israeli threat to Damascus was in an incipient stage. To relieve pressure on the Syrian front the Egyptians speeded up their operations, and their tank forces consisting of two armoured divisions crossed the Canal even before a sufficiently large bridgehead had been established with adequate air defence. Israelis fell into the trap. They wanted to attack the Egyptian armour before it had time to consolidate on the east bank. The Israelis planned an immediate counter-attack before the air defence system could move up. They thought this would also eliminate the Egyptian missile sites covering the Canal Zone. They, however, attempted to first let the Egyptian armour enter the battle and suffer casualties before they launched a counter-offensive which would take them across the Suez Canal. The Israelis felt that their pre-emptive attack against the Egyptian tanks and the crossing operations was likely to be very costly and if it petered out while in the very process of crossing the Canal, there would be serious trouble. The Egyptian attempt to relieve pressure on Syria caused them nearly 200 tanks. It was not until 16 October that Israeli commando units started operating against the Egyptian missile sites followed by a tank bridgehead in the area of Deversoir. The Cairo-Damascus axis made sure that Israel could neither concentrate its forces on one front nor could it achieve a decisive battlefield victory before the super powers intervened. This time Sadat scored many surprises both on the battlefield and on the diplomatic front.

On 16 October 1973 President Sadat came to the National Assembly and announced his willingness to accept a ceasefire on the basis of Israeli withdrawal from occupied territories and to attend a conference under international auspices. That was the time when the U.S. air bridge had practically compensated the heavy losses which the Israelis had suffered and which had almost made them lose balance. Sadat felt that in view of the heavy reinforcements received by Israel it would be unrealistic to carry on war any further. It was tantamount to fighting the USA by proxy he said. Sadat had to a very large extent achieved the political goals he had intended, viz., the vindication of Arab honour on the battlefield and big power involvement in defreezing the situation.

Sadat had correctly anticipated that the Egyptian forces having crossed the water obstacle of the Suez Canal should invite a slow-grinding operation in which the Israeli forces would gradually lose their equipment and momentum without achieving any decisive results and at the same time blunt the edge of their offensive capability. This role was eminently achieved. The rest of the manoeuvres were in response to the requirements of the situation on the Syrian front, a role which was not envisaged with the same clarity but which became inevitable because of the developments on the Syrian front. Sadat realized after two weeks of war that the time had come for continuing the war on the conference table.

8

Vital Decisions

Sadat was shown the Rogers' plan some time in June 1970. He did not think the plan had much to commend itself but in the opinion of Nasser it suited the overall strategy because Nasser needed time to complete the establishment of the missile network along the Canal. According to Heikal, President Sadat went on a secret visit to Moscow on 1 March 1971 with a three-fold purpose. First, he wanted to arrange a joint political and military strategy with the Russians. Second, he wanted Russia to send arms to Egypt comparable to what Israel got from the USA. Third, he wanted to know the quantum of arms supplies and the speed with which he could expect them from the Russians. The Soviet leaders were chary of talking about a joint strategy, but were prepared to give Illyushin capable of launching missiles with the condition that they could be used only after clearance from Moscow. Sadat immediately rejected this condition stating that under no circumstances would he accept any surrender of his own authority.

Nasser's acceptance of the Rogers' plan understandably shook the confidence of some of the Palestinian leaders of the left wing. They considered that Egypt's leaders were tired old men and that young blood should be entrusted with carrying on the struggle to its logical conclusion. Nasser went to great lengths in explaining to Yasser Arafat the reasons for accepting Roger's initiative while there was hardly one per cent chance of it ever succeeding. Nevertheless, Nasser felt that he needed time badly to put the missile defence plan in shape. The military plan for crossing the Canal which by now had taken shape could not be divulged for security reasons, but this was the time when plans had been laid to cross the Canal and make an advance up to the Gidi and Mitla passes.

Nasser invited a meeting of the Arab Heads of States including King Hussein on 22 and 23 September to put a stop to inter-Arab confrontation over the Palestinian question. It was this conference which proved the last straw on the camel's back and the physical and mental fatigue which it involved dealt a final blow to Nasser, who never recovered from it. Nasser stretched his physical endurance beyond limits when he went to the airport to see the Emir of Kuwait off. Such was his state of fatigue that he could not move from the aircraft site even up to his car. By the time he reached home he was taking his last few breaths.

The ceasefire was due to expire on 9 November 1970 and a decision had to be taken about its extension. By now the initial planning for the Canal crossing operations had been completed and had been given the code name Grantie I. The new President had to get his seat and find his way about in his new capacity. The armed forces had to be finally prepared and against the background of Nasser's death 9 November was a bit too early to do anything about the ceasefire except to accept its extension and gain some more time. The acceptance of Roger's plan was no doubt welcomed by the Americans. Any other personality stepping into the shoes of Nasser, they felt, could not withstand Russian pressures.

Sadat's mind was, however, working in another direction. On 4 February 1971 Sadat was to address the National Assembly. He proposed that the ceasefire should be extended by a month and the Canal clearing operations should commence in right earnest. This should be timed with a simultaneous partial withdrawal by Israel to make the Canal traffic secure in implementation of the UN resolution 242. Sadat was thinking in terms of bringing the differences between the U.S. and Israeli national interests to the forefront despite the apparent coincidences in the historical setting.

According to Heikal, Nasser's leverage with the Soviet Union was much greater since Nasser represented not merely Egypt but a pan-Arab sentiment which went beyond the borders of his own country. Strong Nasserite elements had formed blocs in Arab countries such as Iraq, Syria, Lebanon, and Libya.

Ali Sabri opposed Sadat's approach and tried to find support for himself both with the youth as well as within the Arab Socialist Union. Sadat informed the Soviet Ambassador on 22 April 1971 that he was getting rid of Ali Sabri. He informed the surprised Ambassador that it was an internal requirement of Egypt and had nothing to do with Egyptian-Soviet relations. Nasser's charisma was very much still in evidence. Members of the inner circle, such as Sharawi Gomaa and General Fawzi for instance, had believed that they were in touch with the spirit of Nasser through the help of a medium which claimed to speak in Nasser's voice. The spirit was asked various questions through seances whether an attack on Israel should be launched and who the future Prime Minister of Egypt should be and so on.

Sadat meanwhile was more realistic and was attempting to find solid support for his policies within the National Assembly. The members of the inner circle like Ali Sabri and Sharawi Gomaa were also trying to muster support against Sadat. Ali Sabri even accused Sadat during a meeting of the Central Committee of the Arab Socialist Union of trying to interrupt and interfere with his freedom of speech. At that time unity talks between Egypt and Libya were very much in the air, and this became a bone of contention. Heikal, during one of the stormy sessions, tried to restore calm by pointing out that during Nasser's time a conference had been held at Bengazi which was attended by representatives of Egypt, Libya, and Syria and Nasser had supported the idea of unity. Therefore this was beyond controversy. At the suggestion of Sadat a sub-committee was formed to go into the whole question in detail rather than settling such a serious affair in one or two meetings. On 1 May 1971 Sadat acted decisively and relieved Ali Sabri from his post as Vice-President. The lack of any public reaction to Ali Sabri's ouster and the apparently warm welcome which Sadat was accorded at Heliopolis where Sadat and Podgorny had gone in an open car, proved that Ali Sabri had no mass support.

1971 could not be a year of decision because of the internal developments in Egypt and the lack of adequate military preparedness. The military plans were still to be given final shape. Nasser's original plan, i.e., Granite I, was intended to reach the Gidi and Mitla passes. General Sadiq had amended the plan which included further advance from the Sinai passes towards the international borders of Egypt. Subsequently, Granite II was further extended in scope to cover the Gaza strip as well.

Sadat's patience was being exhausted. There was the problem of domestic discord, and he wanted a more intimate Soviet participation in operational plans as well as the supply of weapons and equipment. He therefore wanted to try Moscow once again and arranged a visit to the Soviet capital on 2 February 1972. Interestingly, just before the Moscow visit Sadat had received an offer from Feisal of 20 Lightning fighter bombers bought from the UK This was supposed to be an incentive to other powers such as the Soviet Union to speed up the delivery of offensive weapons to Egypt. The move appears to have had some effect on the Soviet Union which this time agreed to supply TU-22. The Russians also agreed to provide some T-62 tanks.

Qaddafi disapproved of the Egyptian policy. He did not want Sadat to accept Resolution 242 nor did he have much faith in the superiority of TU-22 and T-62. He was also against King Feisal making common cause with Egypt. Qaddafi was also critical of King Hussein over his United Arab kingdom plan proposing a federation of Jordan and the West Bank.

Nasser had realized as much as Sadat did later that strategically it suited the super powers to keep West Asia in a "no war no peace" situation. Israel and the Arabs were in no position to make peace and the super powers were in no position to make war.[1] Thus it suited Israel and the super powers to preserve the status quo. Nasser had tried to get the Soviet Union involved in the West Asian tangle more intimately and feel a certain responsibility for the Arab failures and develop a stake in Arab success. The credit for Israeli successes went as much to the USA as blame for Arab failures went to the Soviet Union. Nasser had therefore accepted Russian advisors down to the brigade level which added up to an impressive total of 20,000. There were as many as 18 Russian air defence teams manning the SAM sites in Egypt. There was a mutual exchange of information between the super powers over West Asia and it became clear when the Israelis turned cautious after the Russian take-over of air defence for a brief period until the Egyptian sites and crews were ready.

Both Nasser and Sadat ensured that while the Egyptian-Soviet friendship served a positive purpose, there was to be no Russian overlordship over purely Egyptian affairs. Whereas certain logistic facilities were made available to the Russian Navy in the port of Alexandria any idea of affording them base facilities in Mersa Matruh on the Mediterranean and at Bernis on the Red Sea was discarded summarily.

Immediately before the October War the U.S. policy was based on the following guidelines. (*i*) They wanted to keep the Russians out of the area and out of active participation in its affairs. This was partly because they objected to Russian presence there and partly because of the risk of a collision between the superpowers which it involved. (*ii*) They wanted to keep the various strands of negotiation separate—to negotiate a settlement between Israel and Egypt, between Israel and Syria, between Israel and the Palestinians (if that ever became possible), and so on, but all separately and not as part of an overall settlement. (*iii*) Each separate settlement should be negotiated stage by stage. (*iv*) Accepting the Israeli thesis, the Americans were convinced that there could be no return to the 1967 borders. (*v*) The Palestine problem was to be looked at purely as a refugee problem. (*vi*) The end result should be a 'Pax Americana' guaranteeing American interests in the area.

Once Sadat became convinced of the inevitability of war he went about it in a businesslike manner. Elaborate security precautions were taken to ensure that the minimum number of essential personnel knew the plan to launch the crossing operations across the Suez Canal. In the conference which was held on 22 August 1973, eight officers from the Egyptian side and six from the Syrian side attended. Those who attended from the Egyptian and Syrian sides included the Ministers of Defence, the Chiefs of Staff, the Directors of Operations, the Directors of Intelligence, and the Commanders of the Navy, Air Force and Air Defence. No minutes of the meeting were kept. Only two copies of pencil notes were prepared, one each for the two Presidents. As a part of an elaborate deception plan Sadat went on a tour of Saudi Arabia, Qatar, and Syria, particularly to the first two, to give the impression that things were normal.

Talking to Heikal some time on 10 September 1973, Sadat stated that many people thought the Egyptians would never fight and war will never come. He said all such doubting Thomases would be proved wrong. It was for the first time that Heikal was taken into confidence by Sadat, who gave him a resume of the complete plan. He said that people were getting a little tired of hearing slogans and the passage of resolutions. Nor was Egypt in a position to seek financial aid from any Arab country unless there was some offensive plan and some activity on the Egyptian side. A "no peace no war" situation was hardly a reason for demanding financial aid. Egypt therefore had to take action and war was the only alternative left.

In order to preserve secrecy Sadat avoided visiting even his own operational headquarters. On 1 October 1973, for the first time the Soviet Union was told, through the Soviet Ambassador Vinogradov, that some moves were in the offing which would try the Soviet-Egyptian friendship treaty. The National Security Council was informed in very general terms that a breach of cease-fire was very likely in the near future. As far as the PLO was concerned, it was only on 1 October 1973 that Sadat invited a group of their leaders and informed them that their cooperation would be required in some sort of action without spelling out the details. On 4 October 1973, Brezhnev informed Sadat that any decision to go to war would be purely an Egyptian decision but if any such decision were taken then the Soviet Union would give the help of a friend. At the same time Brezhnev also suggested the withdrawal of the Russian advisors and their families. Centre No 10, which was the Operational headquarters, was now sealed and no further entry or exit was possible. The persons inside took the oath of "do or die."

The story is best told by Sadat:

According to a set plan, a communique was issued at 2 p.m. announcing that the Israelis had launched aggression against Egypt at two points on the Red Sea and that Egypt was repelling the attack. Although there was no aggression, the communique was considered a diplomatic move, and in breaking the news to the world, Egypt did not consider it a lie because she considered the presence of Israeli forces on Egyptian territory as continuous aggression.

The air force strike was over after twenty minutes and it was a wonderful blow which restored to the Egyptian armed forces their dignity which had suffered a setback in 1956 and 1967. The strike was carried out with 220 planes. According to the estimates of Soviet experts, we were to lose 30 to 40 per cent of planes and be able to hit 30 per cent targets, but Egypt lost only 5 planes i.e., 2 per cent and the strike realised 99 of per cent of its aim. Among the planes lost was the plane of my youngest brother, the late Atef, whom I brought up like my son, and Hosni Mubarak concealed his death and Ahmed Ismail informed me that 5 planes had been lost.

I did not differentiate between my brother and the rest of my sons, i.e., the pilots who were all martyrs and sacrificed their lives to restore the dignity and pride to their motherland. The air strike was hundred per cent successful and this was one of the reasons why I chose Hosni Mubarak to be the Vice President. The air strike put Israel out of balance."

In the first hours of the battle on the afternoon of 6 October 1973 the leading Egyptian infantry faced Israeli tanks on the east bank of the Canal. The Egyptian engineers used great ingenuity in using powerful water hoses to melt open gaps in the sand barriers on the east Bank of the Canal for Egyptian tanks and reinforcements to use in following up the first waves of assault troops. The use of the water hoses was an idea gained from the building of the High Dam at Aswan. There a sand barrier prevented water reaching a hydro electric station. Water hoses were used, therefore, to open a gap in this barrier. The strong water current from the hoses swept the barrier away.

The Egyptian troops used pontoon bridges dating back to World War II to cross the Suez Canal on 6 October 1973. The pontoon took between five to seven hours to put together. This is what the Russians had given us and we had to use them. The Russians had modern pontoons which could be put together in half an hour. They sent us these modern pontoons immediately before the ceasefire, after I had made a strong plea to the Soviet Premier Kosygin. I continued to follow the developments of the battle at the operations room from 2 p.m. on 6 October 1973 upto 7-40 p.m. when I was informed that the Soviet Ambassador in Cairo wanted to have an urgent meeting with me to convey an urgent message from the Soviet leaders. The Soviet Ambassador told me that President Hafiz Assad of Syria wanted a ceasefire within 48 hours.

These details are recorded in the war diary including all the conversations which took place between me and the ambassador or other officials connected with the events in the area.

Non-alignment was one of the principles and aims of the 23 July 1952 revolution. Egypt's position towards the other world countries was often governed by reciprocity and preservation of Egyptian national interest. These developments brought about a cleavage between Egypt and the USA on the one hand and an increased cooperation between Egypt and the Soviet Union. It was said therefore that Egypt was the door through which the Soviet Union wanted to increase its influence in the Middle East. Nevertheless Egypt managed to maintain a semblance of relationship with the USA. The late President Nasser was keen on establishing a personal relationship between himself and President Kennedey and they used to exchange personal messages. This relationship resulted in the aid agreement between Egypt and the USA of the value of $300 million. In spite of the money crisis which cropped up between the two countries the aid continued. Indeed, Kennedey's enemies in America said that through this aid the USA paid for Egypt's war expenses in Yemen.

Israel's aim was to exert pressure to bring about a rupture in U.S.-Egyptian relations. Their agents had planned attacks against the U.S. establishments in Cairo and Alexandria during the early days of the revolution which came to be known as the Lavon affair, which aimed at projecting the revolution as being hostile to the U.S. presence in the area.

Israel's attempts continued in this fashion until they reached a climax during the presidency of Johnson after the assassination of Kennedey. President Johnson started his term of office by sending a message to Nasser asking that the USA be given the right of inspection of the Egyptian armed forces and threatened to arm Israel to guarantee her victory in any war between Israel and the Arabs. In reply to this message, President Nasser expelled President Johnson's envoy, Mr Talbot, from his office, in the year 1965. It was during this year that Israel began preparing for the 1967 war in collusion with Johnson. This confirmed much of what was written at the time about the U.S. stand over the issue.

Johnson gave himself up completely to Zionist pressures in USA and depended on them even for obtaining personal material gains for himself and his family. He endorsed and repeated all the Israeli arguments coined by Tel Aviv as an expression of American policy. Israel said that she was the Amerian military base in the area and that the USA need not establish her own bases in the area as that would incur for her the enmity of the countries of the region.

After the 1967 War relations between Egypt and the USA were severed as a natural corollary of the U.S. stand in the war, and all contacts between Egypt and the USA were snapped. Nasser even utilised the Soviet leaders for contacting Washington on his behalf for any moves which might be made to neutralise the results of the 1967 catastrophe. This did not lead to any results or even hope.

The history of Egyptian-American relations could have continued on its march in its high stride but for an adverse turn which Egyptian-Soviet relations took after the 1967 debacle. Many might not be aware of the fact that Nasser had accepted Rogers' initiative while sitting with the Soviet leaders around the table. He told them that he was forced to accept the initiative because Moscow was not ready to respond to Egypt's arms requirements. Israel on the other hand accepted the initiative because the world had got accustomed to Arab rejection of every attempted solution and she had thought that even Rogers' plan would be rejected by Nasser. Nasser's acceptance of Rogers' plan took Israel by surprise and she quickly changed her stand and rejected the initiative. Israel then started exerting pressure on Rogers.

The first contact between me and Nixon took place on 24 December 1970 when Nixon sent a message thanking me for Egypt's participation in the funeral of the late President Eisenhower. I summoned the then Chief of U.S. interests section, Mr Donald Bergus, and told him that I considered this letter as a new initiative which might open the way for renewed U.S.-Egyptian relations and expressed my readiness to respond to every American step aimed at reconciliation. I also said that if the USA took a hostile attitude towards Egypt the latter would take measures which would make matters worse. I then sent a letter saying that it was time that the USA played her role in settling this conflict. I also stated that the USA in her capacity as a super power was responsible for the continuation of the explosive situation in the area. I added that Egypt wanted nothing more than just peace and that Egypt was aware that the USA was the only power capable of exercising influence on Israel.

On Nasser's death, President Nixon sent Secretary Eliot Richardson to attend the funeral and after his return from Egypt he wrote a report opining that I would not stay in power for more than two or four weeks.

During his first meeting with me, the Secretary of State Dr Kissinger said that Richardson's report was still kept in the State Department files as a historical document so that American officials may not be misled by deceptive appearances or irresponsible information given to them. Rogers visited Egypt on 3 May 1971 and had long talks with me and expressed his surprise at the refined and cultured treatment he received everywhere in Egypt. He said he had come to Egypt with the idea that he would be pelted with eggs, tomatoes, and stones, but he walked through the streets of Cairo and talked to people without being escorted by guards. I said he should not feel surprised because Egypt gave the world culture and civilisation seventy centuries ago.

I did not feel that Rogers was planning to do nothing. I entertained the same feeling towards Sisco who did not show sympathy towards the Arabs. However, later on it became evident that Sisca was only carrying out the policy of the White House and the State Department. After praising Egypt's stand during his visit to Cairo, Rogers shortly afterwards turned against Egypt on account of Israel's pressure which continued until Tel Aviv got rid of him.

Relations between Egypt and America began to take another course after Secretary of State Dr Kissinger took over. He wrote a message expressing his personal interest in meeting any Egyptian official at any level. Agreement was reached that a meeting be held between Kissinger and Hafiz Ismail in October 1972. In spite of this step, he was aware that America would only move within the framework of the prevailing conditions which affirmed Israel's victory and control of the area. Although Kissinger met Hafiz Ismail twice it was fruitless.

When Kissinger learnt about the start of war in Sinai, he thought I had committed a grave mistake and that Israel would wipe out the Egyptian forces and destroy for ever all chances of reaching a peaceful solution. But Kissinger was surprised when Israel asked for America's urgent intervention barely four days after the October War started.

Unfortunately the Arab policies had moved for too long in a groove. It had been a sad tale of lack of unity of purpose resulting in a failure in bringing to bear the enormous Arab potential to achieve Arab goals and restore their prestige, honour, and dignity in the comity of nations. Very often it was too simple to attribute motives to others and indulge in mutual mud-slinging for Arab failures. The Arabs suffered in all respects whether on the military field or on the diplomatic front due to lack of unity. Whereas Israel benefitted every time by the Arab boycott, the Arabs continued to suffer from being forced into a political and military situation not of their choosing. Until 6 October 1973, they fought wrong wars at wrong places at wrong times. The result was a series of disasters, each more devastating than the previous one.

Sadat emerged on the scene like a shining star to make a complete departure from the past and chalk out a path for Arab action which was refreshingly different, well thought-out and well-prepared. For the first time he analysed dispassionately the reason for successive Arab defeats both on the diplomatic and military fronts, and the result of this analysis led him to isolate the basic causes for such a state of affairs. Scoffed at by some critics in Egypt and not taken too seriously by the outside world, Sadat was a cipher before 6 October 1973.

The October War brought about not only a qualitative change in the situation but resulted in a devastating change in the balance of forces in West Asia and ushered in cataclismic changes in the world economic structure through the political use of the great source of Arab power-oil. Every time Arab unity became a reality, the vested interests lost no time in striking hard at various levels to disrupt the ranks once again. Fearful of the consequences of real and palpable Arab unity emerging on the scene, reactionary forces created situations involving regional and zonal confrontation among the Arabs themselves bringing about a split in the ranks both vertically and horizontally as is only too obvious from the events which have taken place in the Arab world since the disengagement agreement was signed over the Sinai.

President Sadat is not new to this game. He has had good innings in the political and military fields over a period of nearly three decades. Time and again he has refused to be blown off his feet by the pressure of circumstances or expediency. While he holds his head high, he has refused to be blown off his feet. He has weathered many storms in the past and every time his strong point has been his unswerving faith in the principles which he holds dear and which are of perennial value. He is not one to play to the gallery, or be a passive creature in the hands of fate and circumstances. He does not choose an easy path nor is he afraid of swimming the currents.

On 16 October 1973 Kosygin visited Cairo when he met Sadat a number of times. Then and during the next three days there was Israeli infiltration into the West Bank which was first not taken seriously due to failures of efficient communication. The full impact of the Israeli infiltration was realized late. This was a situation fraught with political and military dangers. The handling of the situation at this time was indicative of Sadat's characteristic of not being driven into panic. He realized that panic was exactly what the Israelis wanted. The Israelis had expected that the Egyptian high command would pull back all their troops which were east of the canal. Sadat did not fall into this trap. While he stayed put on the east bank he took immediate action to replace General Shazli by General Gamassy.

General Shazli, who was ordered to send a commando unit to wipe out the Israeli pocket in the Deversoir area, had failed to carry out the orders. Shazli either was not well-posted with what was happening on the Deversoir front or he tended to disbelieve the reports which were pouring in about the Israeli build-up. Sadat realized that the time had now come to accept a ceasefire because now the war had entered a stage where detente between the super powers was to be preserved though jockeying for local advantages would continue. In his opinion, this was the time to prevent unnecessary bloodshed because the compulsions of international politics would not permit an outright and crushing military victory against Israel. Observers reported a rift among the Kremlin policymakers with one side recommending more direct and effective support to the Arabs even at the risk of detente and the other section recommending a policy of restrained support within the framework of detente.

Detente was put to a great strain, but it did, however, survive as a pattern governing Soviet-U.S. relations despite the temporary eclipse which it suffered at the height of the campaign. It is significant in remembering that Israel was the first government to accept the Security Council resolution 338. Sadat accepted the resolutions 242 and 338. Syria accepted the Resolution 338 on 24 October 1973. Jordan also accepted it. Only Libya and Iraq rejected the resolution.

The Israelis had accepted the ceasefire only to gain a breather. No sooner was the agreement signed when the Israelis, in a unilateral breach of ceasefire, tried to make gains on the Suez front. This created another explosive situation. Since the situation had now passed on to the enforcement of international responsibility of the super powers, Sadat approached both Nixon and Brezhnev to intercede by sending the required forces to enforce the ceasefire in good faith and prevent violation of it by Israel. A Soviet threat that unless Israel stopped its violations of ceasefire it was going to intercede by despatching troops brought forth a U.S. declaration of a state of alert on 25 October 1973. The Israeli tactics had been to move from one ceasefire to another and make gains in between. It was obvious that between this show of muscle the the super powers sought to perform their assumed roles of international policeman so that when the lines were drawn up pulling the confronting forces apart, each side gained as favourable a position as possible from its own point of view.

The European nations, despite their sympathy for Israel, were made to understand that their industrial prosperity, in fact their very economic existence depended on Arab oil. This realization made them assume an independent stance vis-a-vis the Americans. The vulnerability of NATO was thus exposed. This brought into focus the importance of the Arab-Persian Gulf as the oil-basin of the world. This was the area which in terms of oil controlled Europe and its prosperity. Europe in the West and Japan in the East were dependent totally on the Gulf oil. Sadat realized that the strategic importance of both oil and the Gulf area had been amply demonstrated during the conflict as setting the pattern of the future trend of power balance in the region because in a sense whoever controlled the Arab-Persian Gulf would also have considerable leverage with both Europe and the industrial countries of the far east. This might have been discussed by Sadat during the visit of King Feisal before the launching of the Ramadan War in October 1973. The control of the Gulf depended on the right of entry to it from the Mediterranean and hence the overriding and vital importance of West Asia in the power balance of the world. Thus Sadat had anticipated that the world would move into a stage after the Ramdan War where the solidarity and loyalty of conventional political-cum-miliatry groupings would break down in favour of seekers of oil and economic prosperity.

9

War and its Aftermath

From the point of the intensity of the campaign, the quantum of weapons and equipment used, and the sheer bloodiness of the battles, the Ramadan War has no parallel in history. During the five years from 1967 to 1973 Egypt had spent nearly $9,000 million on the war effort. The endless planning process and the plans Granite 1, 2 and 3 had to come to fruition one day. The day was 6 October 1973 when more than 4,000 guns and mortars on the Egyptian front and 1500 on the Syrian front opened up on Israeli positions. The combination of diplomatic, political, and tactical measures adopted by Sadat to gain surprise succeeded despite Israel's sophisticated intelligence system. The artillery barrage was followed up by an airstrike by 300 aircraft. 8,000 troops in 1,000 rubber boats crossed the Suez Canal in the next quarter hour. Within an hour of crossing, that is, by 15.00 hours, the Egyptian Second Army had captured the forward defence of the Barlev Line. 80,000 troops in 12 hours had crossed over and established themselves 3 to 4 km. east of the Canal by the last light. The progress on the Syrian front was equally impressive.

The Israelis paid the price for their negligence and disregard the Arab armies. The Israeli aircraft flew into the SAM network of missiles, only to be destroyed. The two forward armies had been generously issued with handfired anti-tank missiles the other division having been stripped of them. The Israelis were late in their total mobilisation by 12-24 hours, had not found an effective remedy yet through electronic counter measures and their Barlev Line mentality had cost them dearly. Under the conditions there was no bar to the Egyptian forces extending their bridgehead to the passes. Bridging operations, practically immune to Israeli air strikes, were progressing remarkably well taking as little as 6 hours instead of the usual 12 hours. The Syrian operations aimed at advancing on two axes, north and south, and hoping to link up with the Iraqi and Jordanian columns were progressing well.

It was planned that when the Egyptians reached the passes, the Syrians would reach the Jordan River and Lake Tiberias at the same time and move towards Nazareth. After the initial brilliance of the operations the Syrians lost about 600 tanks imposing caution on the Egyptian advance. Between 9 and 14 October a slogging match ensued resulting in mistakes, misunderstandings and mutual accusations within the Arab camp. Mistaken identity accounted for a few Arab losses and another vital front, i. e., the Jordanian, failed to open across the Jordan river as King Hussain pleaded that he had no adequate air defence and hence Amman itself would be exposed. The Egyptian attempt to relieve pressure on the Syrian front by sending up two armoured divisions met with disaster once it moved out of the missile range. In this confusion, the Israeli infiltration in the Deversoir area was not nipped in the bud and it cost General Shazli his job. The last week of the campaign was a catalogue of ceasefire violations, jockeying for positions, and exploitation of situations by the Israeli command.

Nevertheless, despite the bouts of bad luck suffered by the Arabs during the last week of the campaign, the Ramadan War had released immense forces warranting a reorientation in the world relationship of forces on the military, political and economic fronts. Perhaps there is substance in the criticism that the Arabs, having knocked Israel off balance between 6 to 9 October 1973, failed to capture the passes and dominate the whole of Sinai. This is of course hindsight. Sadat emerged out of this situation as a leader who would observe caution and balance rather than indulge in adventurism with uncertain consequences. However, once the Israelis recovered their balance, there was no alternative but to initiate fresh moves to keep up the momentum of political progress. The result was the "Sinai Agreement. (See Appendix for the text of the agreement.)

There were some counsels within the armed forces of Egypt

who recommended a withdrawal of all Egyptian troops to the West of the Canal. Sadat scotched all such talk as playing into the hands of the enemy. This is what Israel desired. Sadat was firm.

More than anything else it was the Sinai Agreement which invited criticism of Sadat's policy of seeking disengagement unilaterally. The critics maintained that by entering into a unilateral agreement with Israel the other parties to the dispute such as Syria and the Palestinians were left at a disadvantage because it meant Egypt opting out of the war to regain usurped territory. The Israeli parted with the Abu Rudeis oil fields yielding tonnes of oil a year and the Gidi and Mitla passes. The immediate positive gains of Sadat were a greater security for the canal traffic, a stronger military position in the Sinai with her occupation of the vital Gidi and Mitla passes, and access to the Abu Rudeis oil. Egypt, which hitherto received war compensation contributed by Saudi Arabia, Kuwait and Libya could no longer function as the pensioners of oil rich powers dishing out doles. It was galling to the self-respect of Egyptians to continue in this position for long without affecting national morale and dignity. The Israeli government on its part did not have as easy time explaining to its population the turning over of the oil fields and the vital passes to Egypt. Yigal Allon explained that even after the agreement was completed Israel still controlled 90 per cent of Sinai and she was assured of a three-year period of non-belligerency by Egypt so that there could be progress towards a peaceful settlement.

Sadat, who overcame many a storm in the past, faced one more this time. While sticking to his basic position of standing by total Israeli withdrawal from occupied territories and the full support of the national rights of the Palestinians, Sadat insisted that the Sinai agreement was a military and not a political agreement. Egypt could not afford to continue with an uncompromising stand over the West Asian tangle for ever. In order to realize both the national and the Arab objectives it was necessary to move forward from the fossilised positions of past years. Moving in fixed grooves posed the danger of the entire Arab forward movement slipping back into old ruts. The national coffers were under heavy strain. The estimated £ 350 million a year through the Suez Canal had been denied to Egypt ever since the closure of the Canal in 1967. Not only Egypt but international trade had been subjected to a heavy strain because of the resultant 30 per cent increase in the cost of transportation. The guns, tanks and aircraft from the Soviet Union needed spares. Their non-supply ever since the closing stages of the October 1973 War had forced the Egyptians to cannibalise their equipment. Any recourse to a new system of weapons and equipment would need a major reorganisation army training and tactics to keep pace with new acquisitions. A variety of spares needed in that eventuality was not without its attendant logistic complications. Moreover, the search for a new source of weapons and equipment of the required calibre and in the required quantities was bound to be a long one. Taking an overall view Sadat felt that any approach should be a comprehensive approach employing all means—diplomatic, political, military, and economic. It was not enough to merely carry on from war to war and use the intervening period to prepare for a new war. The strategic goal of national equilibrium and economic viability had to be achieved. National life had to go on with a modicum of resources.

Sadat's critics maintained that the Sinai Agreement pre-empted a resource to the battlefield in case of further Israeli intransigence. They said that the agreement would provide Israel an excuse for freezing the situation once again. A three-year respite on the Egyptian front would encourage the Israelis to establish new settlements in the occupied territories to boost the morale at home and stop the ever-increasing exodus from Israel. The critics further thought that the agreement only justified the stand of the rejection front.

On the positive side it could perhaps be mentioned that the difficult problem of the Middle East could be tackled in a series of steps beginning with easier ones and moving on to more complex ones. The Sinai agreement therefore fell into its natural place as being the least complicated of the three major points of dispute, the other two being the Golan Heights and the restoration of the national rights of the Palestinians. The first step of the Sinai agreement released one's full attention towards the Golan Heights and the Palestinians. In this respect Sadat's assessment seems justified. The world body accorded the Palestinians a more or less formal status in its deliberations and the centre of attention also shifted to Syria and the Golan Heights with Sinai out of the way. It is a moot point whether another trial of strength, necessarily limited in scope, will be necessary owing to the compulsions of international power politics to unfreeze the situation once again. In such an event it would be a confrontation whose scope, duration, and venue would be strictly laid down and limited by the super power requirements, and would not perhaps be left to anyone of the contestants. Sir Herald Beeley, a former British ambassador in Cairo said : "It has long seemed to me that the best hope of an eventual settlement would lie in an offer by the United States to conclude a bilateral defence pact with Israel, on the condition that Israel withdrew to the 1967 frontiers with, no doubt, minor adjustments regarded as admissible by Rogers in 1970."

He further observed that the achievement of President Sadat not only in recovering the Sinai passes and the Abu Rudeis oil fields but more remarkably in creating an entirely new relationship with the United States was considerable.

Lawrence Mosher, a Washington journalist said: "Sadat in his eleven-day American visit accomplished what his predecessor Gamal Abdel Nasser only dreamed of doing. He has created a fresh and positive image of the Arab world's most prestigeous spokesman." He further added: "Sadat left the United States with a promise of a nuclear power plant and President Ford's proposed $750 million in economic aid. The White House unveiled its foreign aid package which totals $4.7 billion while Sadat was here. Israel would receive $2.24 billion or 49 per cent of the total but preliminary congressional analysis indicated that new Capitol Hill budgetary guidelines instituted this year would have to be raised by $1.8 billion to accommodate the total sum."

The 8th Article of the Agreement described it as only a step and not a final document. The agreement also stipulated that the concerned parties should continue to bend their energies to bringing about a settlement within the framework of the Geneva Conference according to UN resolution 338. Every agreement which provided for the withdrawal of the Israeli forces from occupied area, no matter how little, should be considered a forward step. Every such withdrawal meant an indirect admission on the part of Israel that her occupation of these lands had no legal or moral validity and that she was required to give them up. The agreement was also intended to give momentum to a movement towards peace so that another stalemate could be stopped from developing. The Sinai Agreement did not go against the spirit of the decisions of the Rabat Summit Conference which disallowed partial political solutions. This did not apply to military disengagements. It could be pointed out that the Rabat Conference was held within five months of the signing of the disengagement agreement between Syria and Israel on 31 May 1974. Neither this agreement nor the one between Egypt and Israel could be interpreted as a violation of the spirit of summit decisions. Israeli withdrawals, however reluctant, were taking place for the first time after 1967 and Israel from now on would be under constant pressure to follow her withdrawals from other fronts and other occupied areas. This also meant that Israel's theories of geographical security and expansionism were untenable in view of the logic of her partial withdrawals. Not only did the Israeli withdrawals indicate a de-freezing of the situation but served to highlight other aspects of movement towards the solution of the problem.

It was mainly at the initiative of Egypt that successive summit conferences at Algiers and Rabat laid down the principles of total Israeli withdrawals from occupied Arab lands and the restoration of the national rights of the Palestinians. Sadat stood by them and continues to stand by them. Ever since January 1975 Egypt presented (even before the disengagement talks were initiated) a plan for the total participation of the Palestinian representatives in the Geneva Conference and presented it to both the Soviet Union and the USA This proposal stated that the Palestinian problem was inseparable from the question of the establishment of a just and permanent peace in the Middle East.

The UN General Assembly by its resolution No 3236 of 22 November 1974, conceded the right of the PLO to participate in the Geneva peace conference as a full-fledged and equal participant. The agreement did not affect the right of individual or collective self-defence in respect of all occupied lands, Egyptian, Syrian, or Palestinian. Sadat made it clear time and again that whereas the Security Council resolution 242 demanded an end to a state of war and a call to non-belligerency, it implied that the ending of the state of war was conditional upon obtaining a peace settlement which took into consideration all ingredients of the disputes. Only if the state of war with Israel ended would she give her ships the right to pass through the Suez Canal flying an Israeli flag and with Israeli crew, whether or not the ships carried civilian goods or arms. Egypt did not touch the question of a state of war while signing the Sinai Agreement. The Israeli Prime Minister Issac Rabin himself stated on 17 September 1975 that the Sinai Agreement did not end the state of war between Egypt and Israel. If one were to draw a balance sheet of the gains and losses of Egypt on account of the Sinai Agreement one could sum up by saying that Egypt gained militarily whereas Israel did not gain any concession politically, legally, or militarily.

The agreement was signed by Israel in September instead of March. The period between March and September was used by Israel to test her influence in U.S. circles and to take advantage of the rift in the U.S. Congress. In March they tried to pressurise the U.S. Congress, Ford and Kissinger. It will be recalled that 76 members of the Congress signed a declaration opposing this agreement. Unfortunately it did not go the way the Israelis liked. Ford stood firm and Jewish pressure did not result in the resignation of Kissinger and Israel decided to sign the agreement in September from a weak position. Even after the signing of the Sinai Agreement, Egypt retained her rights and obligations to ensure total Arab security in accordance with Article 51 of the UN Charter.

SADAT AND DE-NASSERISATION

Sadat's attempts at liberalisation of the regime exposed him to the charge of de-Nasserisation. At a news conference, a Lebanese Nasserist political leader who visited Egypt in April 1974 stated that a meeting of the Arab Socialist Union had been specially convened to exonerate Sadat of de-Nasserising Egypt. The Lebanese leader, Gamal Chatilla, Secretary General of the Lebanese Nasserite Organisation, asserted that Nasserism with its principles and achievements was the symbol of a continuous revolution in Egypt led by Sadat and backed by the people. He went on to say that many individual mistakes had been committed in the press and elsewhere in Egypt but it was unfair to blame it all on the people of Egypt, their institutions or the President of the Republic. (See report in the *Arab World* of 4 April 1974).

There were also some attempts in Egypt to found a second political party in addition to the Arab Socialist Union. Certain Egyptians had wanted to name the new party as "October 6," the date of the great crossing of the Suez Canal. The party was ostensibly to support Sadat's leadership more firmly with all that it signified such as removal of press censorship and the induction of democratic and liberal reforms at home. It seemed that Sadat had settled for breathing new life into the Arab Socialist Union rather than founding a new party. He wanted that the ASU should become a centre of healthy dialogue and a focal point for opposing views rather than rigidly endorse conformism. Immediately after liberalisation student politics in Egypt adopted critical postures and many posters appeared in Cairo criticising Sadat, Nasser, Moscow and Washington. The students, however, acknowledged that with the lifting of press censorship, freeing of political prisoners and the liberalisation of the economy of the country, Sadat had given them unprecedented political freedom.

On 3 April 1974, Sadat made an important speech before the Egyptian students' congress at the Alexandria University and for the first time made unsavoury remarks about Egyptian-Soviet relations. The burden of his speech was that while Egypt appreciated the Soviet support during the difficult hours of war, it did not mean that Egypt had to pay back with her freedom and independence of action. The *Al Ahram* of 4 April 1974 writing in a similar vein stated that Egypt would support the Soviet Union against the imperialists and fight on Moscow's side in any battle of liberation against imperialism, but Egypt would not let any one super power assume control of her internal affairs. He charged the Soviet Union with having delayed the supply of military equipment to Egypt on various occasions until the October War. He contended that the Russians had opposed military moves by Egypt in view of the Soviet-American detente.

Newsweek columnist Joseph Issac said on 19 April 1974 that if Sadat moved towards the U.S., in his opinion the U.S. would have to make Israel vacate the whole of Sinai as a price for peace. Egyptian-U.S. ties were restored on 19 April 1974 and the new Egyptian Ambassador presented his credentials to President Nixon on 19 April 1974. On 23 April 1974 Chancellor Willy Brandt of West Germany also announced his intentions to intensify economic, political, cultural and scientific relations with Egypt. Addressing a news conference Brandt stated that his talks with Sadat had shown a complete identity of views.

An Israeli Cabinet Minister stated on 29 March 1974 that he was doubtful if President Sadat was aiming only at economic development and not war. He, however, conceded that Sadat's speeches since February 1971 had been consistently based on a demand for complete Israeli withdrawal from all occupied territories of pre-June 1967 and the establishment of a Palestinian Arab state in the occupied West Bank of Jordan and the Gaza strip under the leadership of the PLO leader Yasser Arafat.

The Egyptian Armed Forces Supreme Council conferred the "Star of Sinai" on Sadat for taking the October War decision with courage and determination. At the same function the Sinai Star was also conferred on President Assad of Syria. Sadat drove through the packed streets of Cairo in a victory motorcade on 19 February 1974 and proclaimed that five hundred years of defeat and demoralisation of the Arabs had ended. The Egyptian and Syrian forces, backed by the Arab nations had achieved the first real victory in five centuries. He was speaking to a special Parliamentary session convened to honour the heroes of the October War. A famous columnist reported through the *Times* (London) of 14 February 1974:

> Egypt is at an exciting crossroads. With the same determination he showed in mobilizing for war, President Sadat is now mobilizing for peace. Economically, he has launched his programme of national reconstruction—a vital ingredient in his politics of momentum. Politically, he has unleashed the freedom termites to begin their work on what is left of the house that Nasser built. His philosophy is activity and its focal point is the Suez Canal.
>
> There is a lot in President Sadat's favour. For one, his stocks are high. He does not have Nasser's charisma, although Egyptians like his homely style. Most important of all is the way in which he acquitted himself in the October War. This has wiped the slate clean of such haunting memories as the year of decision and the Sinai fog which had done so much to deny him public confidence in the past. Even his critics praise him as a man whose success lies in his actions. Recently Sadat made his post-war intentions clear by giving a definition of his kind of socialism. Its aims, he said, would be 'to guarantee an honourable job for every Egyptian, to secure his present and future, to eradicate hunger, to provide medical treatment when there is sickness, to ensure that he does not suffer humiliation in life

or death and to guarantee that the law safeguards the ruled and not the ruler.'

Despite the mercurial and unpredictable actions of Qaddafi, Sadat maintained a pragmatic and balanced approach to Libya: President Sadat's moderation brought forth a remark by Qaddafi who said, "Sometimes I have spoken harshly to Egypt but that was just because I wanted Egypt to remain steadfast, as the solid fortress of the Arab nations." (London *Times* of 20 February 1974). Qaddafi praised the Egyptian armed forces for their valour in the October War and declared that his faith in Egypt as the Arab bastion had never wavered.

The *Guardian* of 2 February 1974 stated that Sadat had formally assured the Arab world that he stood by two basic conditions for a peaceful settlement—Israeli withdrawal from all occupied territories and the restoration of Palestinian rights. This assurance had been given by Sadat to a Palestinian delegation led by Yasser Arafat on 1 February 1974, and this assurance was intended for general Arab consumption.

There is little doubt that Egypt faced serious economic problems at home threatening her very existence, the chief one being the problem of huge debt payments, resulting from the burden of waging successive wars. Sadat's basic approach was to direct his efforts in a three-pronged drive. Firstly, he attempted to reschedule debt repayment to the Soviet Union, secondly, he tried to obtain economic aid and loans from the USA, Japan, West Germany and France, and thirdly, he attempted to obtain loans and aid from the Arab countries on a bilateral basis. Despite the brave and persistent efforts made by Sadat the results fell far short of his high expectations.

Egypt owed to the Soviet Union a billion pounds sterling which was being paid back by Egypt at the rate of 90 million Egyptian pounds annually in the shape of various products. Sadat tried to reduce the quantum of these instalments so that she could divert some of these products to other countries on payment of hard currency. Egypt proposed to pay 20 per cent of her military debts, i.e. 7 milliard pounds sterling, and 25 per cent of the economic loans (3,700 million pounds sterling) spread over the coming ten years.

The Soviet Union conducted protracted talks in Cairo throughout the month of October 1975 when the Assistant/Director of the Central Soviet Bank insisted on Egypt paying back her debt at the rate of 130 million roubles annually during the first five years, the 120 million roubles during the next five years, increasing to 300 million roubles in the third five-year period and finally 250 million roubles in the fourth five-year period. (These figures were quoted by Mohammed el Sammak in the *El Usbu* of 23 February 1976) Sadat rejected the Soviet proposals just as the Egyptian proposals were rejected by the Soviets and the negotiations between the two parties came to a dead end.

With regard to the loans and aid from the USA most of it was only promised. The USA agreed to forward a loan of 800 million dollars as against 2 milliards and 200,000 dollars given to Israel. West Germany agreed to advance a loan of 245 million marks mainly to finance various plans for development. Japan entered into an agreement with Egypt loaning 54 million pounds sterling towards the widening of the Suez Canal.

As far as Arab assistance was concerned, Saudi Arabia, Kuwait and Libya were to compensate Egypt to the extent of 120 million pounds annually according to the summit decisions of the Khartoum Conference of 1967. However, Libya stopped its contributions after the 1973 War. The Libyan share was as much as 45 million pounds. Despite the abstention of Libya from paying her share to Egypt, Egypt was able to obtain it from other Arab countries, but all this could only meet a fringe of her requirements. In pursuance of the summit conference held in Rabat in the year 1974, Egypt obtained 228 million Egyptian pounds from the Arab countries. Egypt also received 750 million pounds sterling from Saudi Arabia, Kuwait, Qatar, and Abu Dhabi. These four countries agreed to participate in the plan for laying a pipeline for oil, i.e., Sumed from the port of Suez on the Red Sea to Alexandria on the Mediterranean, whose expenses were estimated at $500 million. 50 per cent of the investment was Egyptian for this project. There is substance in the Egyptian view point that these extraordinary economic burdens have been laid at her door on account of her continuing confrontation with Israel in furtherance of the overall Arab cause. She would also expect to be compensated for what she lost in the successive wars or at least her losses in the October 1973 War since the beneficiaries were the Arab as a whole. It was as a result of the war that the Arabs were able to raise petrol prices and reap fabulous amounts as petroleum returns.

1200 million Egyptian pounds was the loss suffered by Egypt in the 1967 War alone in military equipment and civil installations. The civil installations suffered damages costing an astronomical figure according to a report which was prepared by the National Council for Production. In the opinion of this Council the recurring loss accruing to Egypt reached 11,300 million pounds because of her inability to use the Canal and other installations. Had she not entered the war or had it not been forced on her, Egypt would have saved 200 million pounds a year for purposes of development and investment.

During the four years of confrontation Egypt suffered not only materially but also in human losses which it is not easy to compensate. It is therefore ironical that the balance of payment position in the Egyptian budget should show a deficit of 2,400 million Egyptian pounds whereas the Arab income as a result of the price hike in petrol should reach a figure in excess of 120 billion dollars. The Egyptian Prime Minister, Mamdouh Salem in his report to the Egyptian National Assembly stated that Egypt had suffered losses to the extent of 16 billion pounds as a result of the wars of 1967 and 1973. Despite the Sinai Agreement signed in September 1974 Egypt has had to continue to spend large amounts for her military preparedness. The military budget of Egypt for 1976 was estimated at 1 billion and 250 million pounds, whereas the military budget in 1967 was less than half a billion dollars. In accordance with the calculations of one of the members of the Egyptian National Assembly, 16 billion pounds, if distributed among Egyptian families, would fetch 2,200 pounds per family. Sadat's visit to Saudi Arabia was intended not only to obtain Saudi support for her plans but also so that the Saudi example would be emulated by the oil rich countries of the Gulf. The steps taken by the Egyptian government to increase taxes on such items as alcoholic drinks and oil touched only the fringe of the problem.

Sadat saw a real need at present for Egypt and the Arab world to see to what extent they fitted into one another's plans and programmes. The common man of Egypt had suffered and born burdens for far too long and was entitled to ask if he was to be compensated by the rich Arabs. Confrontation depended on military preparedness and military preparedness depended on an ample budget. Indeed Egyptian military preparedness guaranteed her political and strategic influence the Arab world. The issues were all interlinked and called for joint Arab action.

Winding up his week long whirlwind tour of Saudi Arabia and the Gulf countries, Sadat issued a call on 28 February 1976 for an urgent convening of the Geneva Peace Conference to settle the Palestinian question as in his opinion the step by step approach to peace in West Asia was dead. Sadat, while visiting Saudi Arabia, Abu Dhabi, Bahrain, and Qatar, called the Palestinian issue the heart of the matter and therefore the Palestinians should participate in the Geneva Peace Conference. It was not the Sinai or the Golan Heights which were the heart of the problem. King Khalid pledged an immediate aid worth $300 million to Egypt. The UAE also pledged aid whose quantum was not declared.

For those who glibly talk of confrontation it would be worthwhile for them to calculate the astronomical costs of modern war through all its stages of preparation, movement, confrontation, and reorganisation. The figures quoted in this chapter are at best a guide. Added to this would be the time factor involved in absorbing new equipment and techniques in modern war which takes years.

10

The Path of the Golden Mean

Sadat is basically a believer in moderation and the path of conciliation and compromise if it does not come in the way of his principles. Even as a student his conscience revolted against terrorist acts to achieve political goals and he thought society should evolve more rational methods. He considered the challenges of peace more demanding than the challenges of war. He realized that in the present day world of interdependence, rapid communications, and technological advancement, it was necessary to accept the fact of international living and establish contacts with the rest of the world to determine one's place in human society. He surprised the Israelis as much by his diplomatic initiatives as by his military plans. Sadat is no believer in political untouchability.

Immediately after the war, Sadat devoted himself to the economic reconstruction of a war-ravaged country which could brook no delay. The war-worthiness of a nation depended on the economic viability of the country and its economic and industrial infrastructure. Egypt required 4 milliard and 400 million pounds to launch herself economically. It was possible for the three major Arab oil countries to guarantee this amount. Despite the 1973 war and whatever positive results came of it, joint Arab action was still a far cry and there was cleavage in the Arab ranks. In 1973, after the October War, the USA decided to give aid to Israel to the extent of 2 milliard and 200 million dollars. This was a small part of the balance of payment deficit of the Egyptian budget for 1976 despite the fact that the Israeli population did not exceed 3 million whereas the current Egyptian population was 37 million. It was not difficult for the rich Arab countries to give the required aid to Egypt to enable her to overcome this deficit so that the American financial aid to Israel was compensated by the joint Arab aid to Egypt. Israeli-American relations, however, did not bear any resemblance to the intimate blood relationship of the Arabs with Egypt. One of them thought that the rich Arab countries had already fulfilled their obligations to Egypt and to the other confrontation states though it could not be considered complete. One of the reasons advanced for the holdback was that a complete study of the development plans of Egypt and her requirements had not been carried out, but this was a criticism which could apply to all Arab countries. The question of Arab economic assistance and aid was treated and commented upon in a general and vague fashion.

The October War no doubt changed the overall situation in favour of the Arabs despite the current Arab disunity and despite the emergence of the rejection front. In addition to political and military support gained by the Arabs as a whole, one of the major consequences of the war was the rise in petrol prices and a phenomenal increase in the earnings of the petroleum producing and exporting countries. Had there been no war and the enormous sacrifices made by Egypt and Syria in the first instance, it would not have been possible for the Arab countries or the petroleum producing countries to have reaped this enormous profit.

The other side of the coin was that if the petroleum producing countries had not imposed an oil embargo, then the confrontation states would not have gained the political advantages which resulted from the October 1973 War. Egypt, which had taken the leading role in launching herself into war, had not received the compensation to which she was entitled. All aid which she had received since 1973 could not equal the aid which the USA had given to Israel immediately after the October War. The considerable petro-earnings should have led to the assistance of all the Arab countries and not merely one or two countries and should have followed a detailed and comprehensive planning for the development of the Arabs as a whole. Cooperation and aid were based on common interests and any investments should have been based on plans which would bring returns to the investors so that when the petroleum resources of the investing countries dwindled, they could have recourse to self-generating alternative sources of sustenance. Though every Arab country had a right to look forward to satisfactory economic aid from the more affluent countries, the confrontation states had a better right to a compensation by way of the Arab appreciation and recognition for what Egypt and Syria bore on behalf of the Arab cause. The confrontation states had borne a heavy burden not only during the war but over the past twenty years.

The wars in 1948 and 1973 were waged with national participation and with popular support. People readily participated in a war for which adequate preparations were made, so long as they were not misadventures resulting from inadequate appreciation, lack of preparation, and incompetent execution, however noble the cause. In the long run it resulted in considerable loss to the Arabs and affected their overall morale and long-term interests. This is obvious from the Arab-Israeli war of 1948 and that of 1973. Sometimes wars were imposed on the Arabs from which there was no escape and the compulsion of international circumstances made it difficult for a country to extricate itself from war even though she was not prepared for it. This happened to Egypt in 1956 and again in 1967 when Egypt neither intended not had provided for a war situation.

Sadat strived to secure for the Arabs the support of the super powers, now one and now the other, in the same way as the super powers manoeuvred for a better standing with the Arabs. In this effort Sadat sought European assistance in a big way. In any guarantees for the West Asia solution he had expressed the hope that British and French guarantees should reinforce any Soviet-U.S. guarantees about West Asia. Sadat's independent stance secured for him vital aid from France and West Germany. West Germany pledged $90 million in aid to begin with. France made no scruples about selling any weapons to any power against hard cash. In her effort to sport an independent stance, France agreed to afford to Egypt technical assistance in laying the foundations for the production of helicopters under licence. West Germany was sure to provide both the investment capital as well as technology needed by Egypt. Sadat has always had a soft corner for German technology and efficiency.

In Sadat's scheme of priorities the re-shaping of the armed

forces through the diversification of weapons and equipment was a long-winded process which would take its time. Far more urgent was the technical and economic reconstruction of Egypt which brooked no delay. This was so despite the fact that Sadat had said that in another eighteen months the Russian equipment in Egypt would be reduced to junk because of the lack of spares and consequential lack of maintenance of equipment. Sadat concluded a $2 billion deal with France in 1975 for a wide ranging purchase of weapons and equipment. The French President during his visit to Cairo in December 1975 agreed to provide technical knowhow to the Egyptian aircraft and armament industries. It is known that certain armament industries are to be located in Egypt with Saudi Arabia, Qatar and the UAE providing the required capital. Sadat's visit to France in April 1976 was preceded by that of his War Minister General Gemassi. The armament industry, believed to cost $8 billion in the initial outlay, is intended to break the big power monopoly of arms in the Arab world. Sadat's attempt to see Egypt independent and self-sufficient to the extent possible has invited a great number of European arms manufacturers and technologists to participate in the Egyptian experiment.

On 2 April 1976 Sadat visited top security installations at the world's biggest nuclear power plant at Biblis in West Germany. Bonn government sources said that President Sadat has expressed his wish to visit this 1200MW plant where he was allowed access to the top security zone which lies on the Rhine. Rumours had it that West Germany was going to conclude an agreement with Egypt on nuclear technology. All this went to show that while Sadat's military planning was for a comparatively distant future, his economic planning was for the immediate present. Any diversification of weapons and equipment required a considerable period of re-training and adoption of revised technical, tactical, and logistic procedures.

Egypt had a bitter experience in as much as she met with rebuffs first from the United States during the Dullessian era when she withdrew the aid offer for the Aswan Dam, and later when her total dependence on Soviet weapons in the post-1973 years brought her military machinery to a standstill because of her political difficulties with the Soviet Union. In April 1974 Sadat said :

I would greatly welcome a situation where we and the Soviet

Union could stay together as friends and discuss everything frankly. We do not befriend America at the expense of the Soviet Union and we will not befriend the Soviet Union at the expense of America. Whoever offers us the hand of friendship, we offer him the friendship in return. I have taken a decision after consultation with the armed forces to diversify our sources of arms. This has already been implemented. It is difficult for us to stand with our hands tied for 6 months and leave our forces unprotected.

Sadat repeatedly toured the Gulf region because this was the hub of super power attention and activity. Sadat met a number of Gulf leaders and held discussions with them on bilateral cooperation. After a five-day visit to Saudi Arabia from 21 to 26 February 1976, Sadat landed in Muscat for a forty-five minute meeting with Sultan Qaboos of Oman where no one else was present. The talks were reported to have centred round the future of the Gulf region. Sadat's critics saw in this visit a consolidation of the traditionalist elements in the Saudi peninsula and a weakening of the liberation movement in the region. Sadat stated to press men that he would bend his energies to bring about a better understanding between Oman and South Yemen. In reply to another question, Sadat stated that he wanted economic loans from the Gulf countries on a long term basis and that Egypt had suffered a lot economically because of short-term loans as she was forced to pay as much as 20 per cent interest on these loans. He wanted the Gulf countries to start joint plans with Egypt whose dimensions would be discussed in detail.

Sadat's anxiety has been to conduct his campaign at several levels simultaneously to maintain the momentum towards a genuine peace in West Asia without a slide-back into another frustrating "no peace no war" situation. The unresolved issues at the end of the Fourth Arab-Israeli War carried in them the seed for the fifth war. Sadat resolved to build up a deterrent Arab strength encompassing many aspects of national and international life to render the prospect of another confrontation unattractive to Israel.

SALZBURG MEETING WITH PRESIDENT FORD

Sadat described the background to his meeting President Ford in the following words in his *Memoirs*:

> The Israelis had thought the move towards peace had lost its momentum but we were too alert not to let the initiative slip out of our hands and this was the reason for my meeting with the U.S. President Ford at Salzburg on 1 June 1975. The U.S. Head of State was found modest and candid.
>
> In his toast speech at the lunch I gave in his honour at the ancient Futsohel Schloss castle where I stayed at Salzburg, President Ford dwelt on the point that America would not allow another stalemate in the Middle East to develop.
>
> I replied by saying that it was about time firm decisions were taken. America needed no reminder that it held all the cards in its hands as it was the mainstay of Israel in both peace and war. The U.S. was the only country which was in a position to bring decisive pressure to bear on Israel. Such pressure needed a firm decision which America should now take to preserve its great international weightage in the Middle East.
>
> I told the U.S. leader that Israel, despite its total dependence on the United States, surprisingly endeavoured to strike at the American policy in the Middle East seeking to obviate a stalemate and induct a soltution based on justice. It was equally surprising that Israel should deliberately distort the image of America by aborting its step-by-step approach, a policy aimed at escalating the situation.
>
> I told President Ford that Israel feared peace and could not make peace. It had feigned a peace-loving country for well over twenty-six years until the world believed in the fallacy that it was a lamb lost in a jungle of beasts of prey. The Arabs helped Israel's portrayal of them as brutes by refusing any positive steps to win the world over to their just cause and left the field clear for Israel to behave lawlessly at will. Israel thus came to be recognised as a symbol of peace, civilisation and progress while the Arabs suffered the reputation of being bellicose, underdeveloped, reactionary, and destructive despite their just cause.
>
> Israel also managed to deceive the world into believing that its ultimate aim was to be at peace with the Arabs but only when

an Arab leader appeared in the scene capable of signing a peace treaty with her. Israel was now dumbfounded and had lost the trump card it has used over the years to win the world opinion to its side.

Concluding my analysis of the situation, I frankly told President Ford that he faced a real test which, we hoped, he would successfully pass and that his position was very similar to that of President Eisenhower in 1956 at the time of the tripartite aggression against Egypt, which took place only a week before the American elections. The aggression was so timed as to ensure that the U.S. President would be unable to take any decisive action against the aggressors, but Eisenhower, that noble leader, stood firmly not only against Israel but also against Britain and France. Nonetheless, he succeeded in the presidential re-election despite the loss of Jewish votes.

President Ford, commenting on these views, expressed his full conviction that the situation should not be allowed to stagnate whatever the effort required to ensure a continued momentum in the drive towards peace and he suggested another U.S. step-by-step approach.

At this point Kissinger recalled two points, viz., the duration of the disengagement agreement and the early warning (monitor) system which had blocked further progress in the previous round of talks, and asked if there was any hope of some move on the part of Egypt which could enable the U.S. President to have another round with Israel within the step-by-step policy despite Israel's exploitation of the current dispute between the Congress and the U.S. Government.

The existence of Israeli pressure on the U.S. government had taken a concrete shape in the petition submitted by 77 senators to President Ford prior to his departure for Salzburg which called for full-fledged military, economic, and other aid to Israel on the plea that Israel's superiority was the only guarantee for stability in the Middle East.

President Ford said, and I agreed with him, that we should not take a serious view of such things which were common practice in parliamentary life. It was customary that a petitioner collected signatures on his petition, but the Egyptian working group calculated that the real number of American Senators fully sympathising with Israel did not exceed 22 out of the 77 who signed the petition. The rest had their eyes on Zionist influence on the presidential elections.

In respect to Kissinger's request for a new Egyptian move, I said that I was prepared to renew the UNEF mandate on a yearly instead of a six-monthly basis so long as the momentum towards peace continued on the basis of four fundamental demands : (*i*) disengagement on the Syrian front; (*ii*) American guarantee against any Israeli aggression against Syria; (*iii*) Palestinians' participation at Geneva, and (*iv*) convening of the Geneva Conference only after the disengagement had been effected on both fronts.

As for the second point, concerning the monitor system, I insisted that the United States should throw its full weight behind a solution to the problem by making an American offer defining its position thus turning Israel's procrastination into a commitment before the USA which gave it everything from bread to bombs and sustained it.

In order that America should give its full weight to the case and turn from the position of an adversary to a neutral, I asked that it should build and operate an early warning system similar to the set by Israel to report any moves on the front.

The Salzburg meeting was most fruitful and constructive and was a great contribution to the development of Egyptian-American relations. The White House became our friend after twenty years of tense, deteriorating and interrupted relations.

SADAT AND LEBANON

In relation to other problems and disputes, Sadat's approach has been equally moderate and balanced. Some of them bear scrutiny. In an interview with Salim el Lozi, the editor of the Lebanese magazine *El Hawadis* on 3 February 1976, Sadat dealt with the problem of Lebanon and described it as a tragedy greater than that of the formation of Israel as a state. The Egyptian President was sitting in a balcony overlooking the Nile. He seemed to always draw inspiration from a view of the Nile while thinking of serious Arab issues. After narrating the events in Lebanon quickly, the interviewer suggested that according to prevalent opinion the Sinai Agreement did not bring about the intended results because in his opinion this agreement did not emanate from a dynamic and agreed Arab policy. Even the best of the agreements was no compensation for the liquidation of Arab solidarity. The Syrians and Palestinians had accused Egypt of opting out of the war which had weakened the joint Arab stand in respect of Israel. He went to the extent of saying that the Lebanese considered the destruction caused to their country a result of Arab opposition to the Sinai Agreement. But for the agreement Lebanon would not have been subjected to the tragedy of death and destruction.

Sadat said this observation was based on wrong premises and hence the inferences were bound to be erroneous. In his characteristic style for a simple analysis of complicated issues, Sadat said that any person with the least understanding of the problem would not assert that he should not have taken 5,000 square kilometres of Egyptian land from the Israelis, a strip which contained the vital passes and the oil fields. This in fact confirmed the Arab victory in the October War. He disclosed that before the second disengagement agreement in Sinai was signed, he had visited Kuwait, Iraq, Jordan, and Syria to explain the position of Egypt and how he was proceeding in the implementation of the UN resolutions 242 and 338. Sadat went on to say that the Palestinians had assured him that they were committed to Syria geographically whereas they were committed to Egypt politically. Sadat considered the inter-Arab differences a temporary affair. Sadat did not consider that the outburst of violence in Lebanon was an alternative for struggle against Israel. Syrian overlordship of a section of the Palestinians could not be a substitute for responsible joint Arab action either.

In answer to a question Sadat said that every politician in Lebanon was trying to safeguard his own interests in the light of the presidential elections and this gave a different complexion to the essential nature of the crisis. If the Lebanese did not accept Arab help to resolve the crisis then it was inevitable that such help would come from outside in the shape of a summit meeting or in any other form. Sadat described the suggestion that the Lebanese crisis was a by-product of the Sinai Agreement as illogical and absurd. Where was the Sinai Agreement when there was a clash between the Lebanese army and the Palestinians in 1973? Sadat affirmed that Egypt had not opted out of the war and there was no power in the world which could expel it from the war camp. On the other hand if Egypt had been able to open the Suez Canal it was by the use of force. The Israelis were holding the other bank of the Canal and claimed half the water line and even half the Canal dues when it opened. Egypt, therefore, had to fight the October War to push them back to be able to open the Canal. Sadat claimed that his own strategy was based on an understanding of the American and the Soviet strategies and his strategy had the overwhelming support of the Egyptians and a great majority of Arab countries.

THE PALESTINIAN QUESTION

Sadat was not in favour of giving a distinctive label to the PLO forces operating on the soil of Egypt. This attitude was criticised even by some Palestinians but Sadat espoused the cause of the Palestinians consistently and it was through his efforts that the Rabat Summit recognised the PLO as the sole legal representative organisation of the Palestinians. He did much to preserve and protect the Palestinian resistance and effectively interceded on their behalf with King Hussein in March 1972. In January 1971 when a National Conference was held in Aswan, Sadat forcefully pleaded that the Palestinian nation was not a group of refugee camps but a nation entitled to its sovereign national rights. He said that it was not a question of human sympathy but a question of political rights. At the meeting of the Palestinian Council in February 1971, Sadat announced that the Egyptian support to the Palestinian cause was not a reaction to the military disaster which faced her in 1967 but that the Palestinian problem was in his view a movement which signified Arab awakening, politically, socially, and culturally.

In April 1971, while addressing the Islamic Research Conference, Sadat refused to accept the negotiability of either the right of the Palestinian nation for their nationhood or their title to their land. At the second death anniversary of Nasser, Sadat recommended the formation of an interim Palestinian government and announced Egyptian support for its formation if and when the Palestinians chose to form one.

Speaking in the National Assembly in October 1972, Sadat stated that the Arab struggle would never reach its goal except with the Palestinian nation in its vanguard. Again, addressing the National Assembly in October 1975, he stated that the basic foundation of Egyptian action both at the Arab and at the international level was the liberation of all occupied territories and the reversion of the national rights of the Palestinians. He went on to say that there was no land more sacred for the Arabs than Jerusalem, Nablus, Hebron, and Mount Hermon, and that for the Egyptians these were no less than Qantara or Al Arish and this was the basis, he declared, for liberating all Arab occupied lands wherever they happened to be. Sadat sought commitment from President Ford on behalf of Syria and Palestine not in a personal capacity but on behalf of the American government. Sadat went a step further and stated that time was of essential consequence in this respect and that 1976 should be considered as the year of Palestine. He pledged Egyptian effort in securing the recognition of Palestinian needs at all levels and from all platforms. Sadat ensured that before the commencement of the October War of 1973 there was complete coordination between the Egyptian and Palestinian commands which continued throughout the war and later. It is known that Yasser Arafat was one of the very few persons in the top echelons of the Arab leadership who was taken into confidence about D-Day and H-Hour.

Sadat refused to take part in any verbal duels with Palestinian resistance leadership. He refused to recognise the existence of any contradiction between the Egyptian struggle and that of the Palestinians strategically and tactically, and emphasised that their history, struggle, values were common. There were many occasions when the Palestinian movement faced extinction but Egypt stood by it and did what it could to save the movement. When Egypt accepted the Rogers' plan the Palestinian resistance thought it detrimental to its interests. Some Palestinians mistakenly considered the suspension of the Palestinian radio broadcasts from Cairo on 28 July 1970, i. e., shortly before the death of Nasser, as part of the Rogers plan.

Some Palestinian leaders not reconciled to the Sinai Agreement have been called the "Rejection Front." They have criticised Sadat's effort to re-orientate political objectives in terms of economic objectives in inviting the western capital to invest in Arab lands, mainly in Egypt. In their opinion such a step would impose caution on the part of Egypt if war became necessary once again. The "Rejection Front" consists of four splinter groups of the P.L.O., namely George Habash's Popular Front for the Liberation of Palestine, Capt. Ahmed Gibral's Popular Front for the Liberation of Palestine, the Arab Liberation Front supported by Iraq, and the Popular Struggle Front. These Fronts are supported materially and morally by the Libyan President, Col. Qaddafi. They have used some harsh expressions against Sadat, described the Sinai Agreement as capitulation and the U.S. technical team in the Sinai as a U.S. base. They have interpreted the Sinai Agreement as a U.S. attempt to dictate terms not only to the Arabs but also to the Soviet Union and West Europe. The Palestinians were also critical of Sadat's position at the OAU Summit held in Kampala where Egypt opposed Israel's expulsion from the United Nations. While Sadat did so to ensure that some measure of international restraint was operative on Israel if she were a member of the world body, her expulsion would render her unanswerable to any authority, and even the minimum constraints and restrictions on her would vanish. Sadat also felt that Israel's expulsion would, in other words, mean sabotaging the Sinai accord and taking a step in the reverse direction on the path to a political solution acceptable to the Arabs as a whole.

At a time when the Soviet Union has reached an accord with the USA for a technical collaboration and foodgrains deal, Sadat seems to feel that the Arabs should similarly make use of the existing marketing potential and the technical and financial resources of the USA and the West in furthering the Arab economic and technological capacities instead of denying to themselves these advantages. It was this vital factor which lay behind Sadat's bringing about the Arab surplus capital and western technology together in a new relationship where both parties stood to gain. The Soviet Union had not developed a parallel absorptive capacity for the Arab oil and surplus funds in the same way as the West had done. Sadat has been at pains to underline the fact that instead of the Arabs belonging to either one bloc or the other, it should adopt an independent stand to avail of benefits from both blocs in a purposeful system of cooperative collaboration.

The Syrian criticism of Sadat's position stemmed from her objection to the Egyptian commitment to non-belligerency for three years even while most of the Arab areas still remained under Israeli occupation. In the opinion of Syria this adversely affected the Arab cause in general and the Palestinian cause in particular. The agreement had given USA a chance to establish her effective presence in the heart of the Arab land and also allowed Israel a trouble-free southern front so that she could switch over to the northern front with ease and confidence. The Syrian point of view was that when in May 1974 they signed an interim accord on the Golan Heights similar to the one on the Sinai front, it was meant to preserve unity in the Arab ranks. Syria said that she was, in the absence of similarity of views with Sadat, forced to seek a rapproachment with King Hussein and a closer commitment to the Palestinians, both with a view to strengthen the northern Arab front as well as present a deterrent alliance to the Israelis.

Sadat on the other hand claimed that no Arab leader was in a position to renounce war as long as the basic Arab demands were not met, and that if ever it came to fighting another war, Egyptian forces would be in a better position in their revised locations in Sinai than otherwise. While he asked Syria not to provoke a conflict on its initiative, he made it clear that any Israeli attack on Syria would provoke Egypt to renounce the agreement as if it never existed. Both in respect of the recognition of Palestinian rights and an accord on the Syrian front, Sadat claimed to have been assured by the USA in the shape of guarantees given by Nixon and confirmed by President Ford. In fact an American magazine published the details of the secret clauses of the understanding reached between Sadat and the U.S. leaders. The report was not denied by Dr Kissinger who only wondered about the source of the leakage.

Sadat obviously seemed to have appreciated that a stage had been reached in international relations where a commitment to one bloc was outdated if one's national interests were to be pursued with vigour and earnestness. He, therefore, departed from tradition when he visited the USA in October-November 1975. Whatever assistance in training and equipment he was able to draw from the Soviet Union was good as far as it went. The new situation, however, warranted both a liberalisation of the economic set up at home and political affiliations abroad. There could not be permanent affiliations in politics while one pursued national interests. Again, it was not an opportunistic course because the basic Arab demands admitted no compromise. Any rigidity in changing one's style or approach to the achievement of the basic goals was, therefore, one of individual variation. In assessing such individual variations only the results counted.

Sadat claimed that he undertook the visit to the U.S. to promote a U.S.-Syrian dialogue on the one hand and the U.S. recognition of the PLO on the other. Sadat also addressed the UN General Assembly and persuaded it to recognise the PLO's right to be a full member of the Geneva Conference. Syria, however, took umbrage to Sadat pleading their cause in the USA. Sadat's pleading of the Palestinian cause in the international forum tempered the sharpness of Palestinian criticism of the Sinai agreement. Sadat not only warned Israel that its continued occupation of Arab land would leave no other option to Egypt but to go to war again but he also called for the internationalisation of the whole city of Jerusalem.

If on the one hand the confrontation states showed signs of disarray, on the other, the traditionalist countries, particularly Saudi Arabia and the Gulf countries, appeared to have endorsed Sadat's approach to the problem. More importantly Sadat made certain impressive economic gains for Egypt through his policies. The Egyptian economy which badly needed a shot in the arm, received a considerable boost as a result of his visit to the USA, the UK, and France in October-November 1975 and to Saudi Arabia and the Gulf countries in March 1976.

Sadat's economic gains were as follows. President Ford recommended a package aid of $750 million for Egypt as against $740 million economic aid for Israel. Two nuclear reactors of 600 MW capacity were agreed to be provided by the USA to Egypt costing $1.2 billion. This was facilitated by Egypt signing the non-proliferation treaty. According to the "Aviation Week and Space Technology" of 29 October 1975, the U.S. Congress was informed by the administration that U.S. military aid to Egypt would run to about one billion dollars during the next five years. On his return home from the USA Sadat visited London, the first ever visit by an Egyptian President to the UK The Export Group Guarantee Department of London was reported by the *Foreign News and Features* to have sanctioned £ 40 million. The Military Balance also mentioned that the UK had agreed to supply 200 Jaguar planes to Egypt. It made note that Sadat's policies had paid dividends and that Egypt now had 44 Mirages F-1 (French) and 6 Seaking helicopters of British origin.

With regard to Sadat's visit to Saudi Arabia in the first week of March 1976 it was reported tthat while Saudi Arabia desired cooperation between Egypt and Syria, it had sanctioned $5,000 million on behalf of the Gulf states as a whole to Egypt. The proposed aid at the recommendation of President Sadat had been split into two consignments of $2,500 million each. The first was to be in the form of direct loans from individual countries, a $1,000 million from Saudi Arabia, and a total of $1,500 million from Kuwait, Qatar, and the UAE. The second part of the loan was to be collectively subscribed by Saudi Arabia, Kuwait, Qatar, the UAE, and other Arab oil producers.

DE-NASSERISATION

It was natural for the relaxation of press censorship in Egypt to release forces which had somehow or the other suffered during Nasser's time. It was, therefore, natural for such elements to carry out a vilification campaign against Nasser, and they suggested that Sadat's regime was interested in maligning Nasser's memory. This lie was nailed by no less a person than Sadat himself who on the occasion of the second anniversary of the death of Nasser, on 28 September 1972 and also subsequently on similar occasions, forcefully repudiated any such denigration. He described Nasser as an incorruptible and immortal Arab leader who had no personal ambition. The compliments which Sadat paid to Nasser, and the warmth of his love, appreciation, and reverence for the late leader could hardly be hidden. He spoke of Nasser as having given to Egypt an importance in world affairs which it had not had for nearly two thousand years. Nasser was the first Egyptian ruler of Egypt in two thousand years. He did not import alien ideologies and thought structures but revived the best that was in Egyptian culture. The thousands of years of contact which Egypt had with the outside world had imparted to it not only an innate breadth of vision and tolerance but it had also given Egyptian culture depth and confidence. Whether one viewed Cairo or Egypt geographically, historically, or culturally she presented a grand spectacle of the harmonious blending of the ancient and the modern, the Arab and the non-Arab, the transient and the permanent. The tolerance born of this international intercourse left a strong imprint on the thought-structure and the emotional fabric of the Egyptians.

When Rogers visited Egypt he was struck by the warmth of Egyptian hospitality even at a time when political tempers were running high and there was not much love lost between Egypt and the USA. Other dignitaries visiting Egypt were also struck by the abundant Egyptian goodwill. The solid foundations of this nation were derived from a five thousand year old history. This depth was noticeable in Egyptian life if one overlooked the temporary and fleeting appearances of everyday politics. In the opinion of Sadat, Nasser discovered the real elements, the perennial quality of greatness innate in the Egyptians and brought it to the fore.

Sadat has referred to Nasser's attempt to give a practical expression to the Egyptian peoples' natural passion for collective participation rather than the imposition of totalitarianism by a person or a class. In rejecting imperialist threats, particularly the threat of the use of force by vastly superior forces, Nasser only exhibited the inner temper of the Egyptian people. In 1956 Nasser rejected with disdain the Anglo-French ultimatum over the nationalisation of the Suez Canal, and tripartite aggression was unleashed on Egypt. The people of Egypt stood like a rock and Nasser was vindicated in his faith in his people. The imperialists tried to project Nasser and the Egyptian army as being the harbingers of trouble and if they only overthrew the Free Officers they would be delivered. Vast sums of money were spent in buying quislings and hired assassins but all in vain. The paratroop landing in Port Said and the bombardment of the town by Anglo-French forces, instead of causing disgruntlement with the leadership as was expected by the imperialists, only increased the Egyptians' solidarity and identification with their leaders.

When Egypt concluded an arms deal in 1955 with the Soviet Union, the western monopolists and arms peddlars were incensed. They served threats and ultimatums to Egypt. The USA sent a delegate to serve an ultimatum to Nasser but such was the overwhelming personality of Nasser that the delegate did not have the courage even to broach the subject. The London Conference of 1956 chose the Australian Prime Minister Mr Menezes to negotiate with Nasser and serve him a threat, and according to Sadat, "hardly had he uttered the first word about the West and its power, etc. etc. that Nasser closed the paper in front of him and told him that the meeting was over and that he would never accept any ultimatums."

Nasser liquidated class privileges in a peaceful manner in accordance with the innate genius of the Egyptian people and incorporated it in the national charter in 1962. He not only believed passionately in a common Arab destiny but also took positive steps to bring about and establish the Arab unity of his dreams. He brought about a merger between Egypt and Syria and backed the Algerian and Yemeni revolutions to the hilt. The imperialist-backed reactionaries who were ever alert and sensitive to the crystallisation of Arab unity emerging in its progressive ranks dabbled in intrigue to bring about the shedding of Arab blood with Arab swords. This is what happened when reactionaries struck at the unity which emerged between Syria and Egypt. Nasser sensed the underlying currents behind the actions of the reactionaries and wisely accepted with good grace a reversion of Egypt and Syria to their old status and dissolved the unity which had been brought about earlier through a triumphant crystallisation of Arab nationalism. History has turned a full circle and Sadat has been at pains to emphasise that the points of agreement among the Arab ranks should be identified and consolidated more than their differences. In a similar manner Sadat has reaffirmed his basic adherence to the Arab demands about which there is consensus, viz., Israeli withdrawal from all Arab territories and the re-establishment of the national rights of the Palestinians with each party to the dispute evolving its own pattern of approach to this problem taking into consideration its own internal and external situation.

Sadat has mentioned that the charter of the Confederation of the Arab Republics had been drafted by Nasser in his own handwriting before he died. Sadat felt that despite the comments of the cynics and despite the setbacks which Egypt had experienced in her efforts to bring about unity the effort has not been in vain. In a tribute to Nasser, Sadat said: "Thanks to Abdel Nasser, instead of being scattered individuals we have become a revolutionary people and a nation that found itself, controlled its potentialities and nationality, carrying its annals in its right hand and the torch of revolution in its left, a nation which started its drive and will never stop, a nation which will realize, God willing, all its aspirations."

Egypt's First Lady

Egypt's First Lady, Gihan Sadat, has made an in[...] social scene of contemporary Egypt, and has been in t[...] of social reform and social welfare movements in Eg[...] she was a young girl. It would be appropriate to describ[...] the representative of the new urges, hopes, and aspirations of [...] Whereas Nasser's wife was a devoted wife of her illustrious hus[...] and an ideal housewife in the traditional religious concept, Gi[...] with her semi-British background (her mother is of British origin) has functioned as a social pillar of the new Egyptian society. Elegant in her personal appearance, an ideal hostess and highly accomplished lady, she has impressed one and all with her diligence, her attention to detail, and her flair for meticulous and methodical functioning. Because of her social welfare activities and her qualities as an amiable hostess Gihan has come to occupy a very special and revered place in the body politic of Egypt. Her ubiquitous and radiant personality has shown itself in action behind the war lines in the company of wounded soldiers, in hospitals, and at international conferences and social and educational functions. Gihan was educated at the Cairo university and is the mother of four children.

Gihan is forty-two years old and was born in the south of Cairo in the village of Beni Suwaif. Her father, Safwat Rauf was married to Gladys Cotren at Cambridge where the two met. They were married in 1923 and had five children. The couple came back to

Safwat Rauf passed away in 1966.
...ixties and lives a quiet life with her
...ell-versed in Arabic, has embraced
...Fatima. She visits her home in England
Egypt before the birth...
Gihan's mother is...
daughter in Egy...
Islam, and is n... Anwar el Sadat in 1949. At that time Sadat
once a year... the army and Gihan was only sixteen. The
Gihan... ...ence of a Maj. Hasan Izzat who had married
was a... ...n. In 1942 Sadat was fairly active against the
two... Sadat and Hasan Izzat had been arrested for
a... ...t the British. Gihan met her future husband for the
... her fifteenth birthday in 1948 and was highly im-
... Sadat's courage, his patriotism, and his zeal and en-
... for the national cause.

...n had no foreknowledge of the revolution staged on 23
...1952 by the Free Officers. In his book *Revolt on the Nile*
...at has revealed that the night before the revolution he took
...is wife and children to see an open air cinema, accompanied
by Gihan's brother Magdi. When they returned an urgent note
from Gamal Abdel Nasser was awaiting him. He quickly changed
into his military uniform after reading the note and left his home
without an inkling of where he was going. Neither Gihan nor
Magdi had the faintest suspicion that Sadat was taking such a
leading part in the impending revolution. In fact they were the
surprised listeners of the news about the revolution over the radio
for the first time the following morning. The White Revolution
was announced by Sadat over the radio and for the next fifteen
days he did not return home. In a small way this reveals an aspect
of Sadat's personality in that he can keep a secret. The well-known
Israeli quip about secret Arab decisions being available in coffee
houses next morning does not apply to Sadat. Israel paid a very
heavy price for this lapse on 6 October 1973.

Gihan has been devoted to social welfare activities from her
childhood. She took a leading part in organising relief, aid and
assistance whenever and wherever needed long before she
married Sadat. She organised a feminist movement in her village
with the aim of securing rights for women. In the beginning the
ladies who participated in Gihan's movement were those who did
not enjoy perfect conjugal harmony at home. Charity begins at
home. At Gihan's initiative an aid centre was established in the

village to help those neglected women who were unwanted by their husbands and did not have any means of supporting themselves. Gihan procured about twenty-five sewing machines for the aid centre which taught women tailoring and other handicrafts. The products of the centre found a ready market and it is worth recalling that the centre is flourishing even today with the number of machines at 300. Today the centre provides assistance to as many as 3,000 families. It also pays the educational expenses of over a 1,000 school and university students. Gihan still takes considerable interest in the activities of this centre.

Gihan was the first lady to visit the war zone in the year 1967 and organise relief and care for the sick and wounded. Her concern for the welfare of sick and wounded soldiers earned her the nickname "The Mother of Egyptian Warriors." It was at Gihan's instance again that a centre was established under the name of "Faith and Action Centre" with voluntary donations where 300 handicapped soldiers are provided rehabilitation, care, and training. During the crucial Ramadan War Gihan rendered yeoman service with her indefatigable work round the clock in looking after hospitals and other social welfare centres. During 1975 Gihan concentrated her efforts on achieving two objects, firstly, to promote a general awareness among women and the need for family planning, and secondly, to promote literacy among women. Gihan firmly believes that the educated population of any country is its most valuable raw material. By literacy she does not mean merely book learning but a better appreciation of one's legacies. She believes in women's lib but with a difference. She believes in the husband being the traditional head of the family with the wife as his foremost supporter and complement in the family. She believes not in confrontation but in mutual understanding of the respective functions of husband and wife, their mutual trust and equal dedication to the furtherance of the cause of the social values through their adherence to noble tradition. Her activities have secured for her a membership of the village council as well as of the Arab Socialist Union. She is also the President of the Arab African Women's League. She has tried to secure women's rights through the passage of a comprehensive law.

She represented her country in the International Women's Conference held recently in Mexico. Speaking at the conference Gihan stressed the fact that the surest foundation of society was the sanctity of family life. In this women had a key role to play. She warned that women's lib did not mean confrontation, lack of co-operation, opposition, criticism, disharmony and a vicious atmosphere plagued by doubts, suspicion, intrigues and quarrels. She pointed to the existing American society today and made a forceful plea that women should under no circumstances destroy the framework and the basis of the happy life-style of the family. She added that women's lib should be within the overall framework of a country's traditions and cultural patterns.

Gihan addressed the International League for Women where Gihan said with her characteristic candour that so much had already been spoken and written about the subject of women's rights and their liberation that there was no room for adding to this plethora of speeches and writings. She said that basically all human beings should strive for the general welfare of mankind. Struggle for the freedom and equality of women should be within the overall framework of the advancement of human society. She identified the aim of social uplift and the betterment of the human family, to be the creation of a happy and contended family, a well meaning and happy elan and a contended and happy environment. The very fact that it was decided that an International Women's Year be celebrated indicated the fact that happiness, peace, and love were being sought by all humanity and in this search the women of the world had a great and glorious role to play. She said that happiness consisted in being in harmony with one's surroundings, and she believed that women had a vital part in creating conditions of peace and happiness. This was the real aim of International Women's Year. Womens' role was neither one of declaring a war against men nor of stealing a march over them in their specific fields. It was a question of complementary participation and not confrontation.

She recommended that human effort should be directed to fields where it was most needed in an attractive and positive manner. It was futile and self-defeating in her view to waste effort in shouting emotional and artificial slogans. Human energies should not be spent in upsetting the naturality of the man-woman relationship. There was no scope for an unhealthy rivalry or a posture of hostility between the two. One had to create an atmosphere of mutual assistance with both men and women recognising their special fields of work and responsibility.

During the Ramadan War Gihan played a notable role not only in raising the morale of the soldiers but also in encouraging her husband. Heikal says, "She played a gallant part throughout the war, constantly with the soldiers in the hospitals, bringing their cheerful letters and messages to the President which did much to encourage him."

In Sadat's Words

Sadat as a political thinker and social revolutionary has pronounced himself on a number of subjects which are not only of more than passing value but indicate a key to his personality. The following are a few selections.

Democracy
"To combine democracy and the necessary degree of stability in any society is indeed one of the problems facing the entire world today.

The starting point in practising democracy is equality. Democracy should be brought to maturity and it should be rationalised with time. This is the best way in which democracy can be brought to safe harbours. This is the proper way to consolidate our steps and to lead us to a democracy in practice and action not in words and slogans. Despite the fact that the idea of establishing multiple fora within the framework of the Socialist Union has been approved by popular referendum, I decided to form a committee to study the matter in detail. The committee has been formed on as vast a level as possible, comprising all kinds of trends and opinions.

This method will get all into the habit of openly discussing our political problems. Any discussion must eventually come to an end, come to a decision, and no decision whatsoever can be satisfactory to everybody. It is only natural that one opinion should overrule another and it is indeed one of the bases of democracy that we should accept the opinion of the majority until the situation changes with the change in circumstances, and the change itself must take place in a democratic manner. This is exactly what happened in the case we are about to discuss.

No one can claim that the Socialist Union, or that any other institution in the State was above criticism or even violent attack. Yet democracy, as I said, is an outcome of a free discussion which results in an opinion approved by the majority, and we have to accept that opinion, because the democracy we seek is totally different from obstinacy and fanatic biases.

The first point is the need to maintain the formula of the alliance of the working forces of the people; and the need to maintain 50 per cent of the seats on all the active productive boards for the workers and the farmers.

The second point which has emerged from the discussions of the Committee on the Future of Political Action in Egypt is the trend which has refused the immediate freedom of establishing political parties. Everybody knows that the old parties have fallen far back in the process, and that the new parties have not yet attained the proper circumstances for them to take a serious form guaranteeing stability.

In the light of all these factors, our people were right in refusing a direct and immediate return to the freedom of establishing political parties. They were also right in their refusal to return to darkness at this stage which is one of the most critical and delicate stages our country has ever gone through. Moreover, political parties are not built of mirages. Practice itself defines the reality of the historical stage our people are going through, and of the variables that have come upon social relations. All this, taken together, defines the proper cause of political organisation.

The third point in the report of the Committee on the Future of Political Action is the general or public trend; we want to take a definite step forward, a step crystallising various trends representing different opinions in an effective and organised manner, and not in a scattered, dispersed or individual form as is happening now. Only in this way can we clear the atmosphere, and thus all those who have certain opinions or trends will find themselves responsible for a serious and profound study of matters presenting their own efforts and initiatives towards a solution. In that way we can outgrow the simplified attitude of negative criticism to one where we search for disease and remedy at the same time.

There is a great difference between guaranteeing freedom of opinion, within the alliance, in its individual form (which is what is happening now), and between moving forward to a stage where opinions may gather around a forum expressive of them; thus the opinion would have more weight and greater effect and influence. From these fora shall emerge more than one nucleus which would become a point polarizing popular gathering around a particular trend or opinion.

The fourth point reached by the Committee on the Future of Political Action is that there is a clear trend against extravagance in the number of fora. Perhaps it was rightly influenced with what actually happened when forty fora emerged within a few days. I shall permit myself to say that this was unfitting a very serious situation, and is there anything more serious, dangerous, or delicate than setting the first foundation stone for the completion of the democratic structure and political future of the country ?"[1]

The Role of the Armed Forces

"After defending the homeland, the role of the Armed Forces is confined to one very valuable and important matter, and that is to safeguard the Constitution and constitutional legitimacy.

As for the Constitution, the Permanent Constitution, its texts are sacred and stable. They contain what we have recorded in our documents along with that we have acquired from our experience. The Constitution is the father of all laws, and the main cornerstone in the State of institutions. In any country, the Constitution is sacred until amended. Each and every Constitution contains a text explaining the constitutional ways of introducing amendments, i.e., the amendment of the Constitution is explained in the Constitution itself. That is why when I say that the role of the Armed Forces in the alliance is to protect the Constitution, I am imparting a great national responsibility to them, a noble and lofty responsibility. Those who have tried to involve the Armed Forces in matters which do not concern them have discovered the consequences of such an action. We, who have returned the Armed Forces to their true and proper role, have also come to realise that

---

[1] From Sadat's Address to the National Assembly on 14 March 1976.

they have taken over the responsibility of the battle, that they have brought us victory and have turned over a glorious new page not only in the history of modern Egypt but also in the history of our Arab nation and of the entire world.

I say this to remind you that this is the role with which the armed forces started in 1952, with the inception of the Revolution, at a time when the Armed Forces were the avant-garde of the people. You have also heard me say that in 1939-1940, when I started the Free Officers Organisation, I contacted a certain other organisation, the Muslim Brotherhood. I categorically refused the late Sheikh Hassan El Banna's proposal to have our organisation join that of the Muslim Brotherhood. I refused because I wanted to keep a tradition we have continued to respect and that is that the Armed Forces are for the people, all the people, and not for one organisation, nor for one party, class or group."[2]

Head of State

"In this modern age, an age of frequent and rapid action and movement, an age necessitating vigilance, quick action and reaction, quick decisions, the responsibility of a Head of State has greatly increased in various regimes. That is why the ideal position is that which conforms to our values, to our circumstances and to our customs and that is that the Head of State should be free to steer the policy of the State in all its strategic horizons. He should concentrate on the difficult and grave decisions, and should be capable of taking these decisions, with the State institutions, at the proper time and in the proper place. That is why my advice is that there should be no struggle for the post of Head of State in the sense favoured by some, or rather by those who have asked me to allow electoral fights.

The post of Head of State should not be subject to fighting, and no group should be able to use it as a shield or an excuse. The Head of State should only have at heart the supreme interests of the people and of the country, then he has his role as head of entire family. He is the true arbiter between the authorities and the institutions. He is the symbol of national unity and its guardian. When I say that there should be no struggle or contention, I do not mean to choose one person in particular. Certainly not. Yet some

[2] *Ibid.*

have asked for an amendment of the Constitution on the subject of the elections of the President of the Republic, requesting public elections similar to those of the USA."³

Practice
"It is easy to draft the text, but difficult to apply it. We and others have drafted many texts that have remained ink on paper or were spoiled by wrong application that diverted them from their purpose. Many experiments were spoiled by extravagance, in other words, misinterpretation of the text and wrong application of the provisions.

What I am trying to say is that texts are not enough, and that a twisted practice can be harmful. We had the Charter and the March 30 Declaration, and yet before our very eyes the Charter was given a Marxist interpretation. Yet the Charter stipulates the basic differences between our theories and Marxism."⁴

Organisational Form
"The President of the Republic shall be arbiter, so to say, among the various powers and is unbiased. He shall work for the basic, fate-deciding and strategic decisions with the State institutions. In the final analysis, he is the head of the family who shall arbitrate and the safety-valve for everyone. Then come the Institutions—the executive authority, namely the Cabinet in its full power and the legislative power, namely the People's Council with its full powers. Your sessions were a dynamic and magnificent example of constitutional achievement. Then comes the fourth authority, namely the press, which I shall speak of in detail. Other than that we have the Socialist Union which represents the people's alliance and which is the crucible that contains the three fixed fora, the right, the centre, and the left. The President of the Republic is the head of the Socialist Union but his work does not mean that he has power over the fora. The fora should practise political action and present themselves to the next elections with their programmes and their candidates. It is the task of the Socialist Union to protect three points: first, national unity; second, the inevitability of the socialist solution, namely the gains

³*Ibid.*
⁴*Ibid.*

of workers and farmers, free education, equality of opportunity, in other words, the criterion is capacity and efficiency. Third, social peace, in other words, no class or group of the alliance groups should impose its opinion on the other group or classes. The Socialist Union has no power in this, but if a forum errs with regard to one of these three principles, this shall be discussed publicly before the people. This requires that the Central Committee be organised as well as the Higher Executive Committee in order to have the three fora represented in them. The Socialist Union then would be the framework and the crucible, while the fora would be the actual political organisations freely practising their political activities and programmes and proposing their candidates. Once they reach this hall, they shall practise their full constitutional rights."[5]

Sixth Power
"After October 6, the world said that the Arabs had become the Sixth Power in the World, for two reasons: the fighting that took place and the use of the oil weapon.

It would have not been possible to wage the October War except after years of work on my part to re-assemble the Arab nation into one family. Some persons, at present, out of envy and narrow party interests, by means of manoeuvres and outbiddings, are trying to undermine my efforts. But I say to all these people the Arab nation has already taken its place as the Sixth Power in the world. All who make these attempts will drop below. The rest of us will keep our position as the Sixth Power. They will only harm themselves."

Exemplary Society
"If civilisation is one of the basic components for the formation of the exemplary society, Egypt's share will qualify it, uncontestably, to play that part. Its civilisational background has prevented Egypt from indulging in vain-glory, as a civilised society will never fall prey to such defects as they only appear in an upstart and weak society.

The first characteristic of an exemplary society is tolerance and refraining from fanaticism in its various forms, be it racial, reli-

[5] *Ibid.*

gious, or ideological. This particularity is manifested in all its greatness in the Egyptian society where races, cultures and various ideologies have coexisted side by side. The Egyptian people who bear that national responsibility should have a deep-rooted faith in Arab unity. And the Arab unity I mean is not merely raising empty slogans or voicing senseless words totally devoid of context. It is full conviction and a true feeling in the existence of unity between the peoples of the Arab nation with their multiple states and diverse political entities."

Unity
"The unity we speak of is not unity of constitutional forms. Many a unity of this form was established and collapsed in no time, as it was an artificial one, in response to temporary manoeuvres and then turned to mere ink on paper. Had it been a true expression of an objective reality, it would have overcome obstacles, problems, and challenges. Accomplishment of such a unity requires a rapprochement between the various political and economic systems, and the existing social and cultural patterns between two peoples or more. This should be slow and persistent work so that unity comes as the crowning of a national trend and not the artificial outcome of a position, contradictory to reality and truth.

We adopted the inevitable decision of militarily confronting Israel. We eliminated the negative aspects which prevailed in Arab relations. I made of the Arab nation a family once more. We established Arab solidarity on new bases which enabled every single Arab, wherever he may be, to feel that he is part of one entity, and to feel responsible in contributing to and safeguarding this entity. We got rid of the categorisations which separated the Arab states and which wasted much of the Arab and national effort in internal and secondary fights which could only benefit the enemy. When I say categorisations, I mean labels such as reactionary, progressive, and the like. We mobilized all the resources of the Arab nations for the battle, and mainly the tremendous wealth in oil by which our nation, using it in a rational and calculated manner, managed to reach a new international position, and succeeded in imposing its presence as a sixth power respected by the entire world. This was achieved through action and not through hollow words."

The Mecca of Militance

"That is why Egypt has always made it a point to create an atmosphere of openness, thus allowing dialogue on the inside, and open winpows towards the world outside; thus embracing everyone with an idea or a cause, allowing him the opportunity to express ideas and to carry on activities. It is not surprising, then, that Egypt has become the Mecca of all militance in the vast Arab nation, regardless of their ideological or political affiliations, and even regardless of whether they agree or differ in their points of view with what Egypt believes."

Egypt's Achievement

"What else did Egypt accomplish over the past five years? We challenged Israel with peace. Israel had always been accusing the Arabs of refusing to carry the problem from the field of war to the field of peace. Yet the Arab nation managed to lay the responsibility on Israel, and succeeded in proving that the continuing tension in the region was Israel's fault. We succeeded in exporting to Israeli society the disruption which prevailed in the Arab world. We refused to go back to a state of 'no peace and no war'. We carried the Arab-Israeli problem away from the field of polarization of the two great powers. We drew attention to the fact that the American scene should not be left for Israel to occupy. We opened up towards Europe, and called attention to the importance of allowing Europe to play an important role in establishing peace in the Middle East; this led to closer Arab-European relations in various fields. We varied the sources of armament, thus enabling any Arab state to obtain whatever weapons they might need from wherever they may wish, away from any monopoly. We safeguarded the PLO in its capacity as the legitimate representative of the Palestinian people, and defended it against violent attacks from the outside, against sabotage attempts emanating from certain Arab circles seeking their own political interests, which are in contradiction with the line of the PLO We managed to limit any new differences which may appear on the Arab scene, and attempted to solve them so as to avoid any contradiction between two or more Arab states. We refused to interfere in the internal affairs of any Arab state, whatever the temptations, and despite the biased and gratuitous interpretation of this position of ours. Such interpretations were only designed to distort the situation.

On the international level, we defended the right of the Arab States and the States of the Third World to exploit their resources in such a way as to achieve their objectives in the fields of economic and social development. We did not allow international detente to have any negative effects on the Arab situation. We did not allow any break in the solid wall of African support to the Arabs."[6]

Jerusalem
"In my belief, there is not one single Moslem or Christian in our area or anywhere else, who would approve Israel's full sovereignty over the whole of Jerusalem. If there is a proposal for the internationalisation of Jerusalem, such internationalisation should not mean old Jerusalem only but all of it. These are my own views and not those of the Palestinians, who have alone the right to decide what they consider the best for the future of Jerusalem."[7]

Detente
"Now that what is called detente has replaced discord, threat and the resort to means of violence, exploitation and pressure and despite the great difference between the two epochs, the non-alignment movement has been able—after having fulfilled its first mission during the cold war honourably and sincerely—to adapt itself to the new world changes and to play a new fundamental role based on the movement's basic principles. These remain, in my judgment, the true safeguard of people's independence and the freedom of small states which aspire to breathe the fresh air of liberty, to gain control over their natural resources and to advance on the road of progress, away from the spheres of influence. Once this is achieved, they can contribute to the international arena in a significant, valuable, meaningful and effective manner."[8]

The Great Fulfilment
"Today, I would like to proclaim to the world at large that in the name of God and with His blessing, the Egyptian waterway has been completely cleared and purged of Israeli aggression following our glorious crossing of the Canal on 6 October

[6] *Ibid.*
[7] Address to National Press Club, USA, 27 October 1975.
[8] *Ibid.*

1973 and the battles of liberation we fought in defence of our dignity.

It is only natural that this vital Egyptian artery should continue to serve the prosperity of mankind and maintain its universal role of linking together the four corners of the world and promoting trade and interaction among nations and peoples.

The Egyptian, who personifies the goodness of this land, who has dug the Canal through his sweat and blood as a bridge between continents and civilizations, and whose fellow-countrymen have met martyrdom while crossing the Canal to bring peace and security along its banks, is today reopening it to international navigation, and making it, as it was always meant to be, a tributary of peace and a channel to prosperity and cooperation among men.

To those who are struggling for the peace and prosperity of the world and for human progress, Egypt is offering this gesture on its part in order to alleviate the strain on friendly nations and all peace-loving forces."[9]

Nasser

"In his dealings with his nation, Gamal Abdel Nasser did not recognise the boundaries drawn up by imperialism while perpetrating the crime of partition. In this connection, the peoples of the Arab nation have responded favourably to him.

These peoples did not look upon him as an Egyptian leader to whom they would look forward across the barbed wire along borders, but through his love and through a deep faith in his principles and through backing him, these peoples have knocked down all barriers and hurdles. He had gone to the masses of the Arab nation wherever they lived and these masses have followed him wherever he fought.

Gamal Abdel Nasser has gone but his principles will always survive, his banners will always fly high, his struggles will never cease, his nation will never give in, and his victory, with God's will, is certain and will be achieved."[10]

---

[9] Speech by Sadat on the occasion of the re-opening of the Suez Canal on 5 June 1975.
[10] Speech by President Sadat at the Memorial Rally on the death of the late President Nasser, 6 November 1970.

Independence

"We, Egyptians, have lived long on this land and will die on it, as our fathers and forefathers since the beginning of life and as our offspring will do to the end of this world. We will retain our independence and our pride whatever the wounds, bleeding and sacrifice may be, and even if we bleed our heads will remain high and upright."[11]

---

[11]Speech by President Anwar el Sadat at the Assiut University and Upper Egypt's Higher Institute—10 January 1971.

Some Objections Reviewed

It is natural for a man of action and decision to attract bouquets and brickbats from friend and foe. To be objective, therefore, one has to treat both unstinted praise of his conduct of policy as well as an unreserved condemnation with caution. To those who are committed to blocs and ideologies, his actions would be meritorious or blameworthy according to one's predilections. The sole criterion for a balanced assessment, therefore, would be a consideration of the principles of his policy, its general acceptability by the Egyptian and Arab masses, and the consequences and results emanating from it.

Sadat was criticised for asking the Russian advisors to leave Egypt on 6 July 1972 when Egyptian territory was still under Israeli occupation and the promised year of decision had not yet materialised. Later when the war came in October 1973 he was criticised for not fully exploiting the initial military successes thus leaving the outstanding political issues of West Asia as unresolved as ever. Sadat came under a barrage of criticism when he accepted disengagement in Sinai as his earnest for finalising a just peace settlement. It was averred that he had broken the unified Arab front, taken the urgency off the situation by his promise of non-belligerency for three years and even reduced the concern of the USA in forcing or persuading Israel to withdraw from the occupied territories.

It was said that he had, by his over-dependence on the USA

impaired the military posture of Egypt by inviting the wrath of the Soviet Union brought about by the unilateral abrogation of the Soviet-Egyptian treaty of friendship. He had not even demanded a *quid pro quo* from the USA for his cooling off towards the Soviets.

Among other things, Sadat was criticised for giving up the socialist path of Nasser and for encouraging de-Nasserisation of the regime through the liberalisation of press laws and unleashing a venomous propaganda against Nasser. His economic policies at home have been criticised for creating a class of noveau-riche and widening the gulf between the rich and the poor.

To put these points of criticism in their perspective it would help to consider them in the light of some explanations and clarifications offered by Sadat himself and by those who should know. In retrospect it is learnt that Sadat's decision to ask the Soviet technicians to leave Egypt in July 1972 contributed in no small measure to the achievement of strategic surprise in the October 1973 War. Both Israel and the world were lulled into the belief that in view of this move, no major military operation could be launched by Egypt. Since one of the prime considerations of Sadat was to retrieve the military prestige of the Egyptian army through the October War, his action to Egyptianise the army rank and file and de-Russianise them of command and advisory elements is understandable, though it should not be interpreted as an act of defiance against the Soviet Union. In a speech which Sadat delivered on 18 July 1972, he emphasised that the return of the Soviet advisors did not mean that the Soviet-Egyptian friendship would suffer and thanked the Soviet Union for all the help rendered by it. It should be mentioned here that Egypt at no time had any Soviet bases on her soil. The Soviet planes and ships, however, enjoyed the routine logistic facilities at her major air and sea ports.

With regard to his decision to accept a ceasefire and subsequent disengagement in Sinai, it should be remembered that his war aim was not to fight to the last man and last round but to win the twin-objectives of recovering Egyptian military prestige and breaking the political stalemate. Friends and foes are agreed that the Arabs doubtless achieved a strategic victory though in the last phase of the war the Israelis scored a limited tactical victory. The consequences of the strategic victory achieved by the Egyptians and the Syrians were such that none would grudge Sadat the credit for sparking off a major realignment of political, military, and economic forces on the global plane. Sadat's strategic appreciation was that in view of the Super Power detente he had to manage a relationship with them both to yield the best possible results to the Arabs.

Such were the Arab limitations arising from detente that D-day was kept a secret even from the Russians until the war actually broke out. The stakes in casualties were very high indeed and strategic secrecy was well-maintained. Considered against the background of successive defeats and the resulting demoralisation, being the legacy of the Arab armies during the three Arab-Israeli Wars, the degree of success achieved by the Arabs in October 1973 was phenomenal. In view of this, if the Arabs exercised caution and avoided being rash, their restraint is understandable. The view from the other end of the telescope may reveal the wisdom of hindsight but to one who shoulders heavy national responsibilities in the fog of war the view is not all that clear or the choice clearcut.

With reference to the criticism about Sadat not extracting a political price from the USA for his abrogating the Soviet-Egyptian treaty, one cannot but refer to Sadat's own explanation that in matters of principle he did not believe in horse-trading. This view has much to commend itself if seen against the make-up of Sadat's personality, his devotion to traditional, religious, and spiritual values and his adherence to matters of principle rather than expediency. The suspicion that he may have done so at the behest of Saudi Arabia was set at rest by an official denial from the Saudi government. In fact the only reference to the question of withdrawal of the Soviet experts from Egypt found a mention in a conversation between President Sadat and Kamel Adham, King Feisal's brother-in-law as early as the first half of November 1970. Sadat is reported to have told Kamel Adham then that the Russian advisors would be out of Egypt as soon as the first phase of Israeli withdrawal from the Sinai was achieved.[1]

Sadat has been successful in gaining for himself independent political, economic, and military leverage with either super power to further the Egyptian and Arab national interests. The spark

---

[1] *Road to Ramadan*, Mohamed Heikal, Collins, London, 1975, p. 120.

produced by the fourth Arab-Israeli War has, in fact, generated global trends enabling the underprivileged nations of the world to demand a revised pattern of economic existence which would ensure a greater and more equitable share of wealth and of world resources.

Sadat has tried not to let cast-iron prejudices based on ideological and political barriers between the nations of the world come in the way of Egyptian collaboration with any nation, eastern or western. Within the Arab world he believes in the military unity of the countries astride the vertical axis of Egypt, namely, the confrontation states and the political unity of all states lying horizontally from the Atlantic to the Gulf.

In his view Egypt needs to develop a strategic capacity for defence which involved both a long-term plan for laying the basis for defence industries and a short-term plan for diversifying the sources of weapon supplies. The success of this concept, whether in the long-run the technological gap between the Arab armies and their opponent will be bridged or not, cannot be assessed at this stage. Sadat has tried to pool the enormous Arab monetary resources with Egypt's manpower and strategic potential. Will this combination outweigh anything that the Israelis may conjure up? This is for historians to answer in the light of future developments.

In the matter of liberalisation of the press, the first flush of freedom has perhaps encouraged diverse factions to overstate their case and even indulge in personal vendetta but Sadat has made it plain beyond measure that the image of Nasser will ever shine unsullied and untarnished, and his revolutionary ideals will continue to illumine the path of the Egyptian revolution. He has deprecated any tendency on the part of the press to indulge in unsubstantiated sensationalism and unprincipled mud-slinging.

Sadat has reckoned the Egyptian losses in the 1967 and 1971 wars alone as 16 million pounds. Convinced of the need to give his country a sound economic base, he reactivated the Suez Canal on schedule at a gain of $400 million yearly with another $300 million added on account of the Abu Rudeis oil fields. The balance of payments position is showing a deficit of £2,400 million and a debt of £ 2,160 million out of which £ 1,200 million are payable this year. The critics have pointed out to the weakening of the public sector due to the new economic policy, the coming into being of a new class of about 500 noveau riche, and the increase in corruption and bureaucratic red tape. Sadat has initiated a series of measures to combat these negative developments with a vengeance. He is also anxious to build up on the nuclear front.

Foreign investments are coming in but whereas Sadat would like investments in items which would give Egypt self-sufficiency, the investors have other considerations and the gap is not easy to bridge. The divergence in aims remains unresolved. The impact of Sadat's economic policies will be long-range and it would be rash to pronounce judgement on them at this stage.

The other economic asset is the project of the Sumed pipeline linking Suez with Alexandria on the Mediterranean. This project is expected to function with the partnership of four companies—those of Saudi Arabia, Kuwait, Abu Dhabi, and Egypt. This will replace the giant tankers to a large extent. The first pumping is expected to commence in 1977.

The three canal towns of Port Said, Ismailia, and Suez are competing to take the lead in constructional progress. An ambitious plan for Siwa is also receiving attention. The Sinai peninsula which hitherto was considered a barren desert is being connected by underground tunnels with the west bank of the Canal. An industrial zone is to be established in the area. She is collaborating with the Sudan in agricultural expansion as the population of Egypt is expected to touch the 70 million mark in the year 2000. All said and done, the plans when implemented are expected to put the country's economy on a take-off stage. Sadat is only too aware that the nation which has borne successive war burdens and shed the blood of 60,000 of its sons during the last three wars carrying bereavement to practically every family, does deserve to have a breathing spell. Under his leadership the sons of the soil have given their blood and sweat to usher in a tomorrow which promises to ensure for the coming generations not only an honoured place in the comity of nations but also a measure of peace, prosperity and plenty.

Sadat's struggle is essentially based on a broad strategic, political, and economic appreciation of establishing the Arabs as the sixth power in the world. Speaking to pressmen in July 1976 he declared that his aim was to keep the Middle East free from being an arena for super power muscle-flexing. He wanted the Arabs to solve their problems themselves whether in Lebanon or anywhere else, and if necessary through joint Arab action or a round table conference of the Arabs and not at the behest of any power or country. The political solidarity of the Arabs and an economic detente are the main planks of Sadat's post-October War strategy. He has amply demonstrated that he is as much a crusader for peace as a level-headed leader in war.

14

The Future

A proper appraisal of Sadat's policies is possible in the light of the basic interests of the super and other powers in the area and how these would fit in with the national interests of Egypt and pan-Arabism. It would, therefore, be valid to comment on the latter aspect in this assessment. It would be rash to dub Sadat either pro-American or anti-Soviet as these categories do not fit him nor would such an oversimplification explain the complex factors involved in the situation. One thing is certain about Sadat—he is dedicated to serve his country within the larger framework of total Arab interests. In accordance with the dictates of the current-day alignment of forces, some aspects of policy may require to be played down and some high-lighted. This is a transient phenomenon. Mutual interdependence of nations, the need for cooperative endeavour, and the inevitability of co-existence on honourable and mutually acceptable terms are the cornerstones of his policy. This is becoming evident as a survey of recent events would show.

While the rest of the world continued to think in terms of the traditional cold war attitudes, the epoch-making Soviet-U.S. detente initially caught the world napping. During the last two years there has been a greater appreciation of the fact that detente did not mean the end of all conflict but that it induced competitive co-existence with the super powers poised for obtaining a better leverage in regional disputes. Competitive co-existence imparted to the super powers a supervisory role in the control of regional conflicts. The most sensitive region today is the Middle East-Gulf region which has become the focal point of economic-cum-military competition.

The Ramadan War proved that European thinking and attitudes could be influenced through the control of oil in the Gulf rather than military alliances such as NATO. The Western marketing systems, monetary systems, and trade and industry are geared to the Gulf basin. Both oil and the arms industry make up for the sinews of Gulf security. The Soviet moves to counter vested Western interests consist in consolidating the various tiers of defensive rings from Gibraltar extending to the North African coast, the canal zone, the Red Sea, and the Indian Ocean. The land areas of interest would cover Asia Minor, Iraq, Afghanistan and India. They would also be interested in denying to the West the enormous built-in advantages it already enjoys vis-a-vis the Arab oil basin. The Red Sea also controls the African eastern coasts. The strategic bases of the super powers therefore cover the land, sea, and air routes and have become centres of economic, propagandist, political, administrative, and military activities.

The Arabs, Sadat claims, while developing their independent initiatives, have already become the sixth power in the world. He visualises the Red Sea as an Arab lake, the investment of Arab funds purposefully to promote Arab economic power and a long-term Arab arms industry plan with multilateral collaboration. It was at Sadat's instance that towards the end of 1974 the Rabat Summit set up a War Fund of $2,350 million from the oil funds. Again, at his initiative an Arab authority for military industry was instituted on 10 May 1975 with Saudi Arabia, Qatar, and the U.A.E. with a contribution of $260 million each with its headquarters at Cairo to neutralise the defence industries of Israel which manufacture 30 per cent of her requirements.

Sadat is concerned with four basic Arab issues at present. These are the questions of Israeli withdrawal from the remaining occupied territory in Sinai and Gaza, withdrawal from the Golan Heights, the establishment of a Palestinian State on the West Bank, and the internationalisation of the city of Jerusalem. In many ways the solution of every one of these problems is closely interlinked with others. Sadat is realistic enough to see that the facts of history cannot be just wished away. These realities have to be recast in acceptable moulds. The USA is committed to the survival of

Israel but this commitment is not unconditional. Such a survival could be guaranteed by the USA along with other powers after Israeli withdrawal to the agreed borders is carried out. The problem is whether the Arab states, particularly the littoral states, would guarantee Israeli survival. This is where the U.S. could play a useful role. While accepting the facts of history, Egypt had proposed a fifty-year moratorium on Jewish immigration into Israel. Surely in Sadat's calculation the revised role of Israel would impose on her a disincentive to immigration. Sadat's diplomacy wishes to break the vicious circle of immigration, the requirement for an expanded living space, and the consequent aggressive postures to secure defensible frontiers. Sadat's diplomacy aims at reversing this familiar process.

Sadat feels that the Arab-Israeli issue had hitherto been handled to the detriment of the Arabs, and this was acting as an obstacle to the normal economic development of the confrontation states in particular. These states were forced to impose restrictions on themselves much to the detriment of their own economic, social, and cultural development. This unbalanced and sterile policy where the Arab states stood more and more to lose with the passage of time had to be reversed some day.

With regard to the Palestinian problem Sadat advocated for long the formation of a Palestinian government in exile. This would have afforded the Palestinians, in Sadat's view, an opportunity to mobilise formal international support for their cause, while at the same time it would have helped the formation of a nucleus which could gain experience in the formulation of policies and programmes. In Sadat's view it was for the Palestinian leadership to state its demands in clear-cut terms to obviate the criticism that the Palestinians did not have any clear-cut and positive proposals for consideration and that a mere negative attitude could not achieve very much.

As a *quid pro quo* the USA would seek from the Palestinians their recognition of Israel's right to exist within its approved frontiers duly recognised by the confrontation Arab states for a West Bank Palestinian state. Such a package deal would stand a good chance of an initial settlement with credible enough guarantees to Israel to survive without any threat of its being pushed into the sea. Such measures would naturally be accompanied by proposals such as the de-militarisation of areas which would endanger the security of states on either side of the barricade. Mutual suspicion could be further eroded by the induction of massive economic and ameliorative programmes under international auspices to give purpose and content to the economic well-being of the states involved. The economies of the confrontation states faced a big challenge and needed earnest endeavour to become secure.

With regard to Jerusalem, Sadat has recognised the deep emotional attachments connected with this city, not with just a part of it but the entire city of Jerusalem. Sadat has, therefore, recommended the internationalisation of the whole city of Jerusalem.

Sadat's domestic policies of liberalisation in the economic administration of the country and the relaxation of press laws has invited some criticism as being counter to the socialist concepts of the Nasserist era. Sadat on the other hand has claimed that the real aims of the original Egyptian revolution had still to be achieved and one of these was a liberal policy both in the spheres of economy as well as freedom of expression within well-defined limits. Egyptians are today permitted to buy shares in the public sector companies and adequate safeguards have been provided against the sequestration and confiscation of private assets thus purchased. The policy regarding political liberalisation was implemented by Sadat by creating many forums within the Arab Socialist Union where each forum has been given the freedom to discuss the various programmes offered to the country from the leftist, centrist and rightist angles. The forums are to deal with specific economic, political, and social questions, and are not in the nature of independent political parties sporting independent platforms. At the same time the politico-economic measures are dovetailed with world-wide collaboration programmes irrespective of the politics of ideologies.

Liberalisation and all round cooperation is the goal which Sadat has set for himself. His ambitious economic plans are expected to generate world confidence in the political and economic viability of Egypt which is expected to result in her economic resurgence. Those who are prone to think in terms of rigid attitudes such as a break with the Soviet Union and a total dependence on the USA would find the recent events somewhat disturbing. A news agency report of 28 April 1976 stated that the Soviet Union and

Egypt had signed a trade protocol worth £321 million (Egyptian) including £71 million (Egyptian) representing the current year's debt repayment to Moscow. Last year's turnover was reported to be around £360 million. Despite the current phase of Egyptian disenchantment with the Soviet Union, the former cannot afford to ignore either the military equipment received in the past at crucial periods in Egypt's history, nor can a seasoned statesman like Sadat consider Egyptian-Soviet relations as a closed chapter. All that can be said at present is that Sadat does not want to be a helpless pawn in big power politics without the choice of independent initiatives vis-a-vis the militarily and technically advanced powers of the world.

Sadat has confirmed that China had agreed to provide Egypt with spare parts for its equipment from Russia according to a military protocol signed between the two countries on the occasion of the visit of the Egyptian Vice-President, Hosny Mubarak, to Peking. The protocol covered the provision of spares and overhauling facilities for the Mig aircraft. It may be recalled that during the visit of an Egyptian delegation to China earlier, after the death of Nasser, Chou-en-lai had taken exception to the sale of military weapons and equipment by the Soviet Union to Egypt. This was understandable. While the quantum of military aid which can be provided by China to Egypt is doubtful, what is important to note is Sadat's willingness to look beyond political and other barriers between nations and his readiness to negotiate with all to promote Arab interests. It is well known that China's own capability in providing spares and other equipment for the types of Migs possessed by Egypt is limited.

One of the refreshing features of Sadat's policy is to blunt the edge of Iranian-Arab suspicions and hostilities and create a new sense of solidarity among all the powers of the Gulf region in the wake of the Ramadan War of October 1973. He has realised that the resolution of differences between Iraq and Iran over the Kurdish problem, the reduced threat of Israeli aggression and the closing technological gap between the Arabs and Israel, and also the oil interests of the Gulf basin, all point to the need for a reappraisal by Iran of her attitude towards the Arab states. Religious ties also contribute a little to such a reappraisal. Sadat has, therefore, succeeded in enlisting the economic support of the Shah of Iran in the large-scale rehabilitation programmes of the

Canal towns.

As far as the United States is concerned, a new chapter has opened between her and Egypt with regard to military collaboration, which is causing concern to Israel. A $65 million deal under which the U.S. would supply planes and also train Egyptian aircrew has already been finalised. While the various deals have been struck whether for the production or the supply of weapons and armaments, Sadat's appreciation is that an arms build-up, whether conventional or otherwise, has only a limited value in bringing about political changes. Many other factors have entered the field in modern times such as economic strength, technical skill, diplomatic finesse, cultural influence, ideological and racial affinity as the means open to a country to promote her international influence. Sadat seems to be employing these in gaining national goals more successfully than the time-worn method of sliding back on the path of cold war and a stereotyped confrontation on the pattern of what has gone on during the last quarter of a century. Sadat appears to be interested in finding a common denominator whereby it should be possible for the Arabs with their enormous collective economic strength, petroleum resources, and control of vital and strategic areas of the world, to become co-sharers of plenty and prosperity by building up the essential ingredients for becoming a viable power in the world.

Speaking in the National Assembly in March 1976, the Egyptian Foreign Minister Mr Fahmi made an observation that neither the Soviet Union nor the U.S. would liberate the Arab occupied territories and that Egypt would have to depend on her own efforts to achieve her goals. He stated that the termination of the treaty with the Soviet Union would not affect trade relations with it because the latter was importing from Egypt goods worth $80 to 120 million per year in part-payment of Egypt's debts. He also referred to Egypt's efforts to diversify her weapon-system and stated that some major steps in this connection were taken over eighteen months ago. Egypt was obtaining arms even from the countries which at one time had nursed an anti-Arab attitude. Referring to Sadat's policy, Musa Sabri, a columnist, wrote in *Al Akhbar* that Egypt had neither been a Soviet colony nor would it ever become an American colony and that the two giants had agreed to respect each other's interests in West Asia and Egypt, and did not want to stand in the way of the adjustment of interests of the major powers in their areas unless it went against her own interests of development, liberation of her territories, and her own integrity. He emphasised that Egypt bore no enmity towards the Soviet Union nor did she seek an escalation of estrangement with it. Talking of the U.S. he spoke of it as being the power behind Israel but no longer so antagonistic to Egypt as to refuse to understand Egypt's position.

With regard to Sadat's bid to obtain nuclear collaboration both with France and Germany, it is believed by some that the nuclearisation of West Asia would hasten the Israeli withdrawal of occupied territories because the possession of nuclear capabilities both by Israel and the Arabs would produce a balance of terror. The quantum of nuclear weapons in the possession of either side in the West Asian tangle would be immaterial. Israel has no hinterland and has no area to manoeuvre in the event of a nuclear confrontation irrespective of the quantum of nuclear stockpiles. The Arabs by virtue of their larger areas would enjoy a second strike capability which Israel would not have.

Talking about the subject the Egyptian Foreign Minister stated on 30 April 1976 that a balance between Egypt and Israel should be struck not only in the stockpile of conventional weapons but also in the commitment not to acquire or help proliferate nuclear weapons. Both Egypt and Israel would have to accept international constraints on nuclear activities. Mr Fahmi said that no peace settlement could work in the shadow of huge stockpiles of conventional weapons obtained by Israel from the USA. Since another disturbance of balance of power in West Asia would result in unpredictable consequences damaging the long-term interests of the USA and other powers, it should be possible for the USA to bring about a settlement in the area involving the Soviet Union. With the Arabs enjoying the support not only of the Afro-Asian world but also of a majority of the European countries, the USA would be ill-advised to pursue any other course but to seek revised ties with the Arab bloc to preserve her global interests. The fact that Sadat was the first Arab leader of consequence showing willingness to talk peace with Israel points to his confidence and strength in meeting the greatest challenge of West Asia.

Appendices

THE SINAI AGREEMENT

The Government of the Arab Republic of Egypt and the Government of Israel have agreed that:

ARTICLE I
   The conflict between them and in the Middle East shall not be resolved by military force but by peaceful means.
   The agreement concluded by the parties on January 18, 1974, within the framework of the Geneva peace conference, constituted a first step towards a just and durable peace according to the provisions of Security Council Resolution 338 of 22 October 1973, and they are determined to reach a final and just peace settlement by means of negotiations called for by Security Council Resolution 338, this agreement being a significant step towards that end.

ARTICLE II
   The parties hereby undertake not to resort to the threat or use of force or military blockade against each other.

ARTICLE III
   The parties shall continue scrupulously to observe the ceasefire

on land, sea, and air and to refrain from any military or paramilitary actions against each other.

The parties also confirm that the obligations contained in the Annexure and, when concluded, the protocol shall be an integral part of this agreement.

ARTICLE IV

(*i*) The military forces of the parties shall be deployed thus:

(*a*) All Israeli forces shall be deployed East of the lines designated as lines J and M on the attached map.

(*b*) All Egyptian forces shall be deployed west of the line designated as line E on the attached map.

(*c*) The area between the lines designated on the attached map as line E and F and the area between thelines designated on the attached map as lines J and K shall be limited in armament and forces.

(*d*) The limitations on armament and forces in the areas described by paragraph (*c*) above shall be agreed as described in the attached annexure.

(*e*) The zone between the lines designated on the attached map as lines E and J will be a buffer zone. On this zone the United Nations Emergency Force will continue to perform its functions as under the Egyptian-Israeli agreement of 18 January 1974.

(*f*) In the area south from line E and west from line M, as defined in the attached map, there will be no military forces, as specified in the attached Annex.

(*ii*) The details concerning the new lines, the re-deployment of the forces and its timing, the limitation of armaments and forces, aerial reconnaissance, the operation of the early warning and surveillance installations and the use of the roads, the U.N. functions and other arrangements, will be in accordance with the provisions of the Annex and maps which are an integral part of this agreement and of the protocol which is to result from negotiations pursuant to the Annex and which, when concluded, shall become an integral part of this agreement.

ARTICLE V

The United Nations Emergency Force is essential and shall continue its functions and its mandate shall be extended annually.

Article VI

The parties hereby establish a joint commission for the duration of this agreement. It will function under the aegis of the Chief Coordinator of the United Nations peacekeeping mission in the Middle East in order to consider any problem arising from this agreement and to assist the United Nations Emergency Force in the execution of its mandate. The joint commission shall function in accordance with procedures established in the protocol.

Article VII

Non-military cargoes destined for or coming from Israel shall be permitted through the Suez Canal.

Article VIII

(*i*) This agreement is regarded by the parties as a significant step towards a just and lasting peace. It is not a final peace agreement.

(*ii*) The parties shall continue their efforts to negotiate a final peace agreement within the framework of the Geneva peace conference in accordance with Security Council Resolution 338.

Article IX

This agreement shall enter into force upon signature of the Protocol and remain in force until superseded by a new agreement.

UN Security Council Resolution 242 and 338

Text of Resolution No 242 of 22 November 1967

"The Security Council,

Expressing its continuing concern with the grave situation in the Middle East,

Emphasizing the inadmissibility of the acquisition of territory by war and the need to work for a just and lasting peace in which every State in the area can live in security,

Emphasizing further that all Member States in their acceptance of the Charter of the United Nations have undertaken a commitment to act in accordance with Article 2 of the Charter

(*i*) Affirms that the fulfilment of Charter principles requires the establishment of a just and lasting peace in the Middle East

which should include the application of the following principles:
  (*a*) Withdrawal of Israeli armed forces from territories occupied in the recent conflict.
  (*b*) Termination of all claims or states of belligerency and respect for and acknowledgement of the sovereignty, territorial integrity and political independence of every State in the area and their right to live in peace within secure and recognised boundaries free from threats or acts of force.
(*ii*) Affirms further the necessity of:
  (*a*) Guaranteeing freedom of navigation through international waterways in the area.
  (*b*) The achieving of a just settlement for the refugee problem.
  (*c*) Guaranteeing the territorial inviolability and political independence of every State in the area through some measures, including the establishment of demilitarised zones.
(*iii*) Requests the Secretary-General to designate a Special Representative to proceed to the Middle East to establish and maintain contacts with the States concerned in order to promote agreement and assist efforts to achieve a peaceful and accepted settlement in accordance with the provisions and principles in this resolution.
(*iv*) Requests the Secretary-General to report to the Security Council on the progress of the efforts of the Special Representative as soon as possible.

Text of Resolution No. 338 of 22 October 1973
"The Security Council,
1. Calls upon all parties to the present fighting to cease all military activity immediately, not later than 12 hours after the moment of the adoption of this decision, in the positions they now occupy;
2. Calls upon the parties concerned to start immediately after the ceasefire the implementation of the Security Council resolution 242 (1967) in all of its parts;
3. Decides that immediately and concurrently with the ceasefire, negotiations start between the parties concerned under appropriate auspices aimed at establishing a just and durable peace in the Middle East."

Select Bibliography

Mohammed Anwar el Sadat (in Arabic), Haundi Lutfi, Dar ul Maarif, Cairo, 1972.
Sadat—Five Years of Travail (Record of Speech in Arabic, 28 September 1975), Ministry of Information, A.R.E.
Nasser—The Cairo Documents, Mohamed Heikal, New English Library, London, 1972.
Revolt on the Nile, Anwar el Sadat, Allan Wingate Ltd., London, 1957.
Confrontation, Walter Laqueurm, Wildwood House and Sphere Books, London, 1974.
The Land and People of Egypt, Zaki Naguib Mahmoud, J.B. Lippincott Company, Philadelphia and New York, 1959.
The Road to Ramadan, Mohamed Heikal, Collins, London, 1975.
Nasser—The Man and the Miracle, Dewan Berindranath, Afro-Asian Publications, New Delhi, 1966.
The Ramadan War (in Arabic), Major General Hassan el Badri, Egyptian General Writers' Organisation, Cairo, 1975.

Index

Abyssinia, agression on, 33
Adibin palace incident, 21, 26
Ahmed Oralu Pasha, 25, 28; resentment against, 17-18
Aid Centres, establishment of, 122; functions of, 123; Mrs Sadat's role in, 122-123
Al Ahram, comment on Egyptian-Soviet relations, 98
Alexandria, British attack in 1882, 18; Russian Navy in, 81
Ali Maher Pasha, removal from Premiership, 37-38; role of, 43
Ali Sabri, 66; removal of, 79
Amr Iban al Aas, role of, 17
Anglo-Egyptian Treaty of 1936, Nasser's view, 33, 35; signing of, 46-47
Arab Heads of State Conference, 78
Arab nationalism, 44, 120; Khruschev on, 55-56
Arab Socialist Union, 8, 64, 67, 71, 79, 97, 98
Arab Summit Conference, 6, 59, 61
Arab-European relations, 133
Arab-Israeli war, 58; analysis of, 72-73; Arab defeats in, 86-87, 92; Barlev Line, 11, 75; Cairo-Damascus axis, 76; casualties, 75, 139; ceasefire, 76, 78, 89; consequences of, 105-106; Dayan's suggestion, 10; defreezing of, 5; Egyptian armed forces setback in, 82-83; Eisenhower's views on, 110; expenditure in, 91; Ford's comment on, 111; Israeli air raids, 70; Israeli infiltration into the West Bank, 88; Israeli infiltration in the Deversoir area, 88, 92; Israeli positions in the Sinai, 74; Israeli theory of security, 73-75, 96; Jarring's proposal, 10; losses, 83, 102, 140, 141; Rogers' Plan, 78, 85; Sadat's achievements, 139-140; Sadat's discussion with Kissinger on, 111; Sadat's diplomacy in, 145-146; Soviet air defence missile in, 70; Super Powers role, 4-5, 9, 73; 80; UN resolution on, 78, 89, 95-96, 112; US policy, 81; war in Sinai, 86-87.
Arab-Persian Gulf, importance of, 89-90
Arabs, sixth power, 131, 141, 144
Arafat, Yasser, PLO leader, 99, 100, 114
Army, British Military Mission advice to, 33; dissatisfaction in the ranks of, 17; Egyptianisation of, 16; General Masry's proposal for recognition of, 35-36; prestige of, 138; reorganisation of, 16, 94, 106-107; role of, 4, 128-129; technical competence doubted by the Soviet Union, 9; withdrawal from Merga Matruh in the western desert, 38
Assad of Syria, 99; visit to Cairo, 9
Aswan Dam, 83; US failure to construct and Soviet promise to help, 55, 107

Ayoubid dynasty, 14
Aziz el Masry, Egyptian Chief of Staff, removal of, 37; and the Germans, 36; as the tutor of King Farouk, 36; Sadat on, 30, 40

Baghdad Pact, 4; Egypt's reaction, 53
Balance of payments, 140
Balkan War of 1912-24, General Masry's role in, 30
Bandung Conference and Egypt, 54
Beeley, Sir Herald, 95
Bengazi, evacuation by British, 42
Bernis, Russian base at, 81
Bir Hakim, occupation of, 42
Boumedienne, Houari, visit to Cairo, 62
Brezhnev, 73, 84, 89
British-Military Mission, 33

Caliph of Baghdad, authority of, 13
Centres of power, liquidation of, 61, 71-72
Chou-en-lai, 146
Churchill, Winston, 38, 53
Confederation of the Arab Republics, Charter of, 120
Constantinople Convention of 1882, 12
Constituent Assembly, 65
Constitution, 65

Damascus, Israeli threat to, 75
Dayan, Moshe, on Arab-Israeli war, 74; theory of open bridges, 69; suggestions of, 10
Defence aid, 54, 55, 80, 119, 147
Defence budget, 102
Defence industry, emphasis on, 144; Chinese aid, 147; setting up of, 144
Defence Plan (Plan 200), 79, 80, 91; discussion on, 61-62
Democracy, Sadat's view on, 126-128
Development projects, 140-141

Dhofar province of Oman, revolt in, 10
Dulles, 51; anti-Communist phobia, 51-54

Egypt, achievements of, 133-134, 138-142; and Algeria, 62; and China, 55, 147; and France, 100, 106-107, 117; and Japan, 100-101; and Jordan, 69-70; and Libya, 67-68; and Saudi Arabia, 68-69, 101, 102, 108; and Soviet Union, 4, 9, 54-56, 67, 77, 78-79, 80-81, 85, 98, 100-101, 145-146; and Sudan, 8-9, 67-68; and Syria, 9, merger between, 120; and U.K., 54; Israel's role in sabotaging, 84, 87; and U.S.A., 4, 54, 84-87, 95, 98, 100-101, 107, 109-110, 116, 118-119, 148; and Yemen, 56; and West Germany, 98, 100, 101, 106, 107; Anglo-French-Israeli aggression on, 4, 51, 55; Anglo-French intervention in Government of, 17; British attempt to bring Turkish rule in, 15-16; British imperialism hold over, 4; British occupation in 1882, 19; British protectorate, 20; debts, increase of, 17; deficit budget, 105; economic and military position under Sadat, 117-118; economic reconstruction of, 104-105, 140-141; economy of, 70-71, 98, 102, 100-101; end of Ottoman rule in, 15; fight against British imperialism, 4; farmers' condition in, 34-35; historical background of, 3-4; independence of, 22; Italian interference in, 33; Mameluk rule in, 14; people of, 14; population of, 105, 141; role in Arab world, 3; social structure on the eve of the II World War, 34-35; strategic importance of, 3; trade relations of, 147; Turkish minority in, 18
Egyptian civilization, 3; history of, 13-15

Index

Eisenhower, 53, 110; Egypt's participation in the funeral of, 85
Emir of Kuwait, 59, 60, 78
Exemplary society, characteristics of, 131-132
Export Group Guarantee Department of London, aid to Egypt 117

Fahmi, 148
Family Planning, Mrs Sadat's role in, 123
Farooqian monarchy, 45
Farouk, king, 34, 39, 54
Faud, king, British support to, 32; death, 32
Fawzi, General, 79
Fiesal, King, 10, 59, 60, 68, 80, 89
Ford, US President, 95, 97, 109, 114, 116
Free Officers Constituent Body, formation of, 46
Free Officers Movement, 39, 40, 46, 128; and German High Command contact between, 40; distribution of secret bulletins, 35-36
Freedom movement, 4
Fuka, evacuation of, 42

Geneva Conference, PLO's right to participate, 95-96, 103
Gulf region, importance of, 144

Hassan Izzat, 40; arrest of, 122
Heikal, Mohamed, 77, 81, 125, *Nasser—The Cairo Documents*, 1, 53
Hosny Mubarak, visit to Peking, 146
Hussain el Shafei, 29, 66
Hussein, king, 75, 78, 113; and Gulf countries, Sadat's role in conciliation between, 70; and 1967 war, 69; Sadat's opposition of his plan, 69-70
Hussein Mutawalli, 35

Intellectual movement (1880s), 19-20
International Women's Conference, Mexico, Mrs Sadat's role in, 123
International Women's Year, 124
Iraqi-Soviet friendship, 10
Israel, arms supply from France to, 54; birth of, 44, 46; and the western camp, 52; theory of security, 73-75, 96; super powers commitment to the survival of, 4; US aid to, 104, 117; US recognition to, 45
Islam, cultural values of, 19
Islamic Research Conference, 113
Islamic Summit Conference, Sadat's role in, 6
Italian fascism, rise of, 33

Jafar Numeri, campaign against, 8-9; visit to Egypt, 67
Jamaluddin el Afghani, role of, 19
Jarring, proposal of, 10
Jews Corps, establishment of, 45
Johnson, 84
Jordan and Palestine, clashes between, 9, 69

Kennedy, 84
Khalid, King, 103
Khedive, resentment against, 17-18
Khartoum Conference of 1967, 101
Kissinger, Henry, 97; 111, 116; on Arab-Israeli war, 75; on Sinai agreement, 11, on Sinai war, 86-87
Kosygin, 83, visit to Cairo, 88
Khruschev, 55
Kurdish problem, 146

Lavon Affair, 55, 84
League of Nations, 33
Lebanon crisis, Sadat's role in, 111-113
Libya, Italian interference in, 33, 37, 38
Libya-Egypt unity, 79, 100; opposition of, 66

London Conference of 1956, 55, 119

Maneluk dynasty, and Turkish authority, 14
Meir, Golda, on Arab-Israeli war, 74
Menezes, Australian Prime Minister, 119
Mersa Matruh, 30; evacuation of, 42; Italian forces towards, 38; Russian base at, 81
Mohammed Ali, contribution of, 15-16, 44
Musa Sabri, on Sadat's policy, 147-148
Muslim Brotherhood, 37, 49, 129; aim of, 48; founding of, 48
Muslim society, modernism in, 19
Mussolini, attack on Libya, 38
Mustafa Kamal, role of, 19
Mustafa Nahas Pasha, as Prime Minister (1936), 32; visit to London, 32-33

Napoleon, 19; against Ottoman rule, 15
Nasser, Gamal Abdel, achievements of, 51; and Kennedy, 84; and Rogers' plan, 77-78, 85; and Sadat, 53; architect of post-revolution policies, 53; instructor of the Military Academy, 43; leader of military revolution group, 40; as President, 51-52; as President of Society of Free Officers, 34; assassination attempt on, 51; death of, 1-2, 10, 52, 59-61, 78; death anniversary of, 113, 118; education, 29; exile of, 35; international policy of, 53-55; leverage with the Soviet Union, 78; meeting with Khruschev, 55; posting in Sudan, 39; removal from Mankabad to Alamein, 39; role of, 33; Sadat's views on, 135-136; *The Philosophy of the Revolution*, 58
Nationalism, growth of, 4, 19-20

Nationalist movement, 20-21
Nationalist Party (1907), rise of, 19
Neguili, General, 53
Nehru, Jawaharlal, 56-57
Newsweek, comment on US-Egyptian relations, 98
Nixon, 89, 116
Non-proliferation Treaty, Egypt's signing of, 117
Nuclear capabilities, 149
Nuclear power plant, plan to build, 107, 141; US aid for, 95
Nuclear stockpiles, 149
Nuclear technology, agreement with West Germany on, 107

"October 6", plan to form new party, 97
Oil embargo, imposition of, 105
Oman and South Yemen, understanding between, 108
OAU Summit, Kampala, Palestinians' reaction, 115

Palestinian question, 78, 81, 96, 100, 103, 120, 133, 145-146; and Egyptian resolution, 45; Arab mistakes, 45; charges against, 45; documents on, 45; Egypt's contribution, 113-118; guerrilla warfare against the British, 45; national rights, recognition by West, 7; representation in the UN, 7
Palestinian Arab state, establishment of, 99, 144
Paris Peace Conference, 20, 22
Petrol prices, rise of, 102, 105
Podgorny, visit to Egypt, 67, 79
Port Said, bombardment of, 51
Presidential elections, 61, 62, 63, 65
Press censorship, removal of, 98, 118, 138, 140

Qaddafi, Col., 67-80, 80; praises Egyptian army, 100

Index

Rabat Summit Conference, 95-96, 113, 144
Rabat, Sadat's colleague, 26
Rabin, Issac, on the Sinai agreement, 97
Ramadan war, 56, 70, 73, 75-76, 89, 90, 144;
Red Sea, importance of, 144
Revolution of 1919, 27-28; beginning of, 21
Revolution of 1952, 2, 4; aims, 50
Revolutionary Command Council, 5, 34, 36, 37, 53, 57, 65
Revolutionary Group, plan of, 49
Richardson's report, 86
Rogers' Plan, 77-78, 85, 86; Palestinian resistance to, 114
Rommel, 37, 40, 42
Royal Intelligence Services, 36

Saad Zaghloul, death, 22; exile, 22; role of, 20-21
Sadat, Anwar el, achievements of, 7; address to the UN General Assembly, 117; analysis of his policies, 143-149; and Ali Sabri, 79; and de-Nasserisation, 97-103, 118-120, 138; and Hassan el Banna, 49-50; and Kamel Adham, 139; and King Fiesal, 10, 68, 80, 89; and King Khalid, 10; and Masry, 30-31, 36-38; and Nasser, 30, 46, 53, 134-135; and Qaddafi, 67-68; arrest of, 38, 41, 122; as chief executive, 10; as leader of civil revolutionary group, 40; as Minister of State, 56; as a soldier, 51; birth, 22-23; broadcast, on Nasser's death, 1-2; childhood, 26; Commission in infantry, 29; compliments to Nasser, 118-119; contribution to the non-aligned countries, 6; criticism of, 137-138; decision to go to war in 1973, 4, 10; differences with Nasser, 64-65; early years of, 24-25; economic and military aid under, 117-118; economic policies of, 104-105, 140-141, 146-147; education of, 23, 24, 26-27, 40; editor of *El Gomhouria*, 56; escape from prison, 38, 41; family background of, 23, 50-51; hatred for imperialism, 27; influence of revolution of 1919, 22, 27-29; leadership of, 18, 141; letter to Brezhnev, 73; letter to Khruschev, 56; marriage of, 122; meeting with Ford, 109-110; meeting with Kosygin, 88; member of the Society of Free Officers, 34; *Memoirs*, 2-3, 71-75, 109-110; Nasser's views on, 50; on detente, 134; on democracy, 126-128; on Egyptian civilization and culture, 23; on Egyptian-Soviet relations, 98; on Egypt's achievement, 133-134; on exemplary society, 131-132; on Jerusalem, 134, 144, 146; on liberation of the Sinai, 23; on powers and responsibility of Head of State, 129-131; on Rogers' Plan, 77; on student demonstrations, 23-24; on Arab defeats, 87-88; on the role of the armed forces, 128-129; on Soviet help, 107-108; on unity, 131; patriotism and statesmanship of, 6; personality of, 3, 11-12; post-war strategy of, 142; policies of, 7-9; political philosophy of, 48-49; plot against the British by, 122; pro-west and anti-Soviet criticism of, 6; removal from army, 42-43; return to the army, 46; role in Lebanon crisis, 111-113; role in the Ramadan war, 75-76; *Revolt on the Nile*, 36, 50, 122; revolutionary activities of, 41-42; Secretary-General of the Islamic Conference, 56; *Time* magazine's comment on, 5-6; village life of, 24-25; visit to Bangladesh, India and Pakistan, 6; visit to Gulf region, 108; visit to France, 107; visit to Saudi Arabia, 81, 102,

108; visit to Soviet Union, 9, 55-56, 77, 80; visit to USA, 95, 116; visit to West Germany, 107; western media propaganda against, 71; white revolution announced by, 122; willing to accept ceasefire, 76; youthful days of, 24

Sadat, Gihan, address to the International League for Women, 124; aid centres established by, 122-123; childhood, 122-123; education, 121; emphasis on literacy among women, 123; family background of, 121-122; marriage, 122; on women's lib, 124; president of the Arab-African Women's League, 123-124; role during the Ramadan war, 125; welfare activity of, 121, 123, 125

Safwat Rauf, death, 121

Salah Abdul Sabur, *The Story of the Contemporary Egyptian Conscience*, 19

Saudi Arabia, and Egypt, 68-69; and USA, 68; contribution to the Arab struggle, 68-69; monetary resources of, 68-69; political and spiritual importance of, 68

Secret revolutionary society (1939), 33

Shaarawi Gomaa, 62, 63, 66, 79

Shazli, General, removal of, 88, 92

Sinai agreement, 11, 87, 92-97, 111-116, 138, 150-152

Sino-Egyptian relations, 147; recognition of, 55

Siwa Plan, 141

Social realism, growth of, 19

Social reform and social welfare movements, Gihan Sadat's role in, 121

Socialism, 99

Society of Free Officers, development of, 34

Soviet experts, removal of, 70, 71, 73, 80, 137-139

Soviet-Egyptian Treaty of Friendship, 67, 82, 138, 139

Soviet-US detente, 71, 88-89, 98, 134, 139, 143

Soviet-US food accord, 115

Sudan, 8, 9; Anglo-Egyptian administration in, 18; as place of exile for Egyptian officers, 35; crucial period for, 67; Egyptian rule over, 18; political violence and British Government's reaction, 32; revolution of 1885 in, 18

Suez Canal, Anglo-Egyptian agreement on, 51; British troops in, 33, 47, 53; British troops withdrawal of, 51; ceasefire, 47; clearing operations of, 78; closure and impact on economy, 70-71; Dayan's suggestion, 10; Egyptian forces in, 2-5; nationalisation of, 55, 58; reactivisation of, 140; Sadat's reaction of Dayan's suggestion, 10

Suez Canal Company, shares of, 17

Syrian-Egyptian unity, dissolution of, 58, 96

Third World, 11

Tobruk, fall of, 42

Wafd Party, 21, 32, 33

War expenditure, 91

War Fund, setting up of, 144

War College, role of, 29

Wasifi el Tel, Jordanian Premier, murder of, 69

Weapons and equipment, long-term plan for diversifying of, 7, 8, 94, 140, 144

World War, first, 4, 20; second, 4, 34

Yemen, Nasser's campaign in, 68

Yemeni revolutions, Nasser's support to, 120

Zakaria Mohieddin, 66